It's All About You,

Jesus

It's All About You,
Jesus

A Fresh Call to an
Undistracted Life

Fawn Parish

OLIVER
NELSON™

THOMAS NELSON PUBLISHERS
Nashville

Published in Nashville, Tennessee, by Thomas Nelson, Inc.

Unless otherwise noted, Scripture quotations are from THE NEW KING JAMES VERSION. Copyright © 1979, 1980, 1982 by Thomas Nelson, Inc., Publishers.

Scripture noted The Message taken from *The Message:* The New Testament in Contemporary English. Copyright © 1993, 1994, 1995. Used by permission of NavPress Publishing Group.

Scripture quotations noted TLB are from *The Living Bible,* copyright 1971. Used by permission of Tyndale House Publishers, Inc., Wheaton, Illinois 60189. All rights reserved.

Library of Congress information

Parish, Fawn, 1958–
    It's all about you, Jesus : a fresh call to an undistracted life / Fawn Parish.
      p. cm.
    Includes bibliographical references (p.).
    ISBN 0-7852-6612-7
      1. Spirituality—Christianity. 2. Spiritual life—Christianity. 3. Jesus Christ—Knowableness.
I. Title.

BV4501.3 .P37 2001
248.4—dc21

2001031495

Printed in the United States of America

3 4 5 PHX 05 04 03 02

This book is affectionately dedicated to my clear-faced friend, Carey Nosler. Carey, you have been like Jesus to me, faithful and true. You've poured your life into the prayer movement in this region, doing all the work, while I received all the credit. Your devotion to the simplicity of Christ, hard work, and attention to detail has given me courage to explore new possibilities in seeking to turn faces toward Jesus. The Father honors you, Carey, and I join Him. May you completely be for time and eternity all about Jesus, and may your tribe increase.

Contents

Preface

When I was young, I enjoyed something that may strike you as peculiar. I attended a church that was across the street from a well-known cemetery. Many famous people were buried there. During the one hour we had to ourselves each Sunday, between services, orchestra practice, and a couple of rest home meetings thrown in for good measure, I loved to roam the cemetery and read tombstones. I was fascinated by the way people would sum up a life in a sentence. And, of course, I always wondered what sentence would be used to sum up my life.

Recently I came across a couple of sentences that will more than do. Lesslie Newbigin has been called one of the greatest Christian thinkers of the twentieth century. He was the Bishop of Madras, a missiologist, author, and astute cultural assessor. At the Bishop's funeral several years ago, Rev. Dan Beeby said about Lesslie: "He knew everybody and talked easily with the great, but easiest with the humble, poor and lost. *When he dropped a name, it was always the name of Jesus.*"[1]

I cannot think of anything more meaningful to be said of a life. At the end of my days, that is exactly the sort of comment I'd like people to make about my life. This book is about that kind of life, an undistracted life where Jesus is our first word, our last word, and all the words in between.

There is no greater joy for the Father than when His Son is honored. On the following pages we will explore ways to restore Jesus to the heart of all our stories. Where Jesus has been in the "tiny type" in our lives and religious endeavors, we will seek to give Him the prominence the Father has given Him. When Jesus is the heart of our thought lives, our relationships, our devotion, our story to the world, we will find people drawn to Him. For no matter what we have tried to make it, history is really His Story. God has always intended His Son to occupy the center stage of history. This holy ambition of God begins with Jesus' occupying center stage of our lives. It's always been about Jesus. It's never been about us or anyone else, and it never will.

St. Augustine wrote of Jesus: "Late it was that I loved you, beauty so ancient and so new, late I loved you! . . . You called, you cried out, you shattered my deafness: you flashed, you shone, you scattered my blindness: you breathed perfume, and I drew in my breath and I pant for you: I tasted, and I am hungry and thirsty: you touched me, and I burned for your peace."[2]

I invite you, loved one, to respond to this fresh call to an undistracted life. May Jesus shatter our corporate deafness. May His brilliance scatter our blindness. May He never be merely first in our lives, but be our *very* life, our every breath. May you pant and hunger and thirst for Him and burn with holy, sacred fire.

One

It's All About You, Jesus

A Christ supplemented is a Christ supplanted.[1]

—WILLIAM HENDRIKSEN

You would have worried had you been his mother. He was scrawny, the kind of kid other kids make sport of mocking. A decidedly unhurried learner, school bored him. He was a terrible test taker, and had celebrated his eighth birthday before he could even read. But by making one incredible decision, he was welcomed to a seat at history's table. Augustin Jean Fresnel's[2] life is more than just a great story, a curious paradox, a tale with unexpected twists and turns. Augustin's decision has immense significance for every lover of God.

AUGUSTIN'S DECISION

Had you been a sailor in Augustin's day, you would have lived a fairly short life. Lighthouses could not project light out to sea far enough to warn oncoming ships. Ship captains often did not see the light until it was too late. The bones of ships cluttered the beaches of the world. The problem was not for lack of well-placed lighthouses, *but for lack of light being reflected far enough out to sea.*

For two thousand years people explored ways to correct the problem, finding little success. Starting with the lighthouse of Alexandria, built around 280 B.C., until the eighteenth century, lighthouses saw very little improvement in their ability to project light. It was not because people were not trying. Most concentrated on developing better fuel. People thought if they could just make the flame brighter, the problem would be solved. Wood, coal, whale lamps—nothing proved effectual. The breakthrough came two thousand years later, when Augustin Jean Fresnel made an important decision. Instead of trying to improve existing lighthouse technology *or* producing better fuel, *Fresnel would study the behavior of light itself.*

Fresnel did not study lighthouses. His focus was not on design, maximum configuration, and placement. He would not exhume the ribs of fractured ships and do a doctoral thesis on flawed ship construction. He never wrote a manual on lighthouse maintenance and staffing. Instead, (and this is the crucial point of this book), *he spent his life studying light itself.* And for thousands of ships and sailors, that made all the difference.

Fresnel, using the properties of reflected light, was able to cast a beam out to sea for twenty miles. His studies in light later became the principles used in automobile headlights and in the flashing lights on police and emergency vehicles.

By studying the behavior of light itself, Fresnel solved the mariners' problem. Fresnel became the father of modern optics. His story illustrates a compelling reality for the people of God. *It is more meaningful to study the character of Light Himself than to concentrate on any other thing related to Him.*

We face the same problem faced in Fresnel's day. We have light, splendid light, *but it is not reflected far enough out to sea to alter the course of people's lives.* Lives, marriages, and institutions shipwreck daily and land sundered, bleached, and rotting on our shores. Daily, our culture is battered on the razor-sharp edges of postmodernism and relativism. Yet we persist in ineffectually tending the light, hoping to warn a few ships to turn toward deeper waters.

A Generation Adrift in Churning Seas

The casualties are enormous. We are a compassless generation, adrift in fiercely churning, lightless seas. In my nation, a six-year-old child recently pulled a gun in a kindergarten and shot another six-year-old student to death. Around the same time in California, an eighteen-year-old girl dumped her dead premature son in the neighbors' garbage can and will not be prosecuted. Pick up any major newsmagazine and read the manifest of shipwrecked lives. There is no question about it. We are a generation seriously adrift, breaking up on the hidden reefs of faulty ideologies. Charles Colson observes,

All the grand propositions advanced over the past century have fallen, one by one, like toy soldiers. The twentieth century was the age of ideology, of the great "isms": communism, socialism, Nazism, liberalism, scientism . . . all the major ideological constructions are being tossed on the ash heap of history. All that remains is the cynicism of Postmodernism, with its bankrupt assertion that there is no objective truth or meaning.[3]

We are like the *Titanic* plowing full steam ahead into pitch darkness. We even wonder if such a thing as light even exists.

JESUS, THE FIRE-CORE OF THE UNIVERSE

In the midst of our peril, we are not strangers to hope. Into this pitch-black night enters Jesus, the Light of the World. His light pierces this despairing generation's angst. His kingdom's advance is relentless. His light shatters the long night. He has not diminished a single watt of His luminescence. He is blazing with the light of a thousand suns. The Lamb, who is the Light, illuminates the entire kingdom of God. The light of Life penetrates all darkness. In His gaze nothing remains hidden. Literally blazing with the glory of His Father, Jesus lights the skies. Darkness cannot comprehend Him. Where He is, all things are clearly seen. In His Light, we see light. He is, as George MacDonald says, *"the fire-core of the universe,* the first and the last and the Living One."[4] He is the centerpiece of all life. He is the Light that lights every man who comes into the world. The Light is not, nor will it ever be, the problem. Jesus is completely and utterly sufficient. *Yet, He has chosen to be seen through the lens of our lives.* We are barely reflecting Him because we are not focused on Him. Where are the Augustins who will concentrate solely on knowing Light? Our greatest need is a return to the simplicity of devotion to Jesus. We are aware that countless ships are colliding in the night. We know the statistics. We have seen the skeletons on the beaches. We have a problem and it is this: the children of Light are not focused on Light Himself. We are concentrating on many things *related* to Him, but we are not focused *primarily* on Him. The main thing is no longer the main thing. Or perhaps I should say, the main One is no longer the main One.

TINKERING WITH SPIRITUAL TECHNOLOGY

Like lighthouse engineers through the centuries, we are daily seeking to improve the amount of light that radiates out to sea. We exhaust our energies, tinkering with spiritual technologies and techniques, looking to anointed people or effective practices. We are heavily invested in finding things that work. We have a plethora of spiritual options available: church growth studies, contextualization, spiritual mapping, prayer case studies, warfare methodologies, city-taking strategies, reconciliation initiatives, city transformation models, cultural engagement mandates. The list is growing and instructive. We live in a communication era of instant cross-pollination of significant research and ideas.

Never before has the universal church been able to be on the same page at the same time, learning to pronounce, together, new vocabularies. The possibilities for mobilizing the people of God toward united objectives are enormous. God has gifted the church with stunning tools and information.

We can now stratify, categorize, and quantify what works and what does not. Our research and ideas now find a worldwide audience instantly. This creates a creative synergy that can lead to massive breakthroughs. Our ability to connect globally and immediately has led to the creation of specialties, and new spiritual technologies, that delight and amaze.

Surely, we think, these new approaches will cause the light to increase. We have pastoral unity advocates, revivalists, cultural redemption proponents, Christian worldview futurists, family values lobbyists, warfare specialists, prayer specialists, city-taking strategists, prophecy specialists, doctrinal purity specialists—but *we have increasingly fewer people concentrating solely on studying the personality and character of Jesus, the Light.* Our light is not reflecting and penetrating far enough out to sea because we are focusing the lens of our attention on good things, but not on the most vital thing: Jesus Christ, the Light of the world.

We are in serious danger of obscuring Jesus through our myriad specialties and spiritual options. A. W. Tozer observed that just as the scientist lost God amid the wonders of His world, he feared evangelicals were about to lose God amid the wonder of His Word.[5] I would add that in our generation, we are about to lose God amid the wonder of new spiritual technologies and spiritual options. With their impressive and dazzling capacities, they often obscure the very One they were designed to clarify.

JESUS AND WALDO

Have you ever opened a *Where's Waldo* book? Inside is page after page of thousands of people, all of whom look very much alike. Your task as a reader is to find the hidden Waldo. An untrained eye can spend a good twenty minutes looking at any page of the book before finding him. Like finding Waldo, sometimes locating Jesus in the current landscape of Christendom takes a lot of serious concentration.

Jesus is often no longer the preeminent part of the presentation because Jesus is often the presumed subject of the sentence. Industries have sprung up around Him. Many of these ministries started out as cottage endeavors and quickly evolved into empires. Many of these empires are run by good, well-intentioned people. There are no malicious intentions, no underhanded conspiracies. Jesus is in the picture all right, but like Waldo, He is not the preeminent part of the presentation. Often He gets the six-point type (similar to the type credit card companies use on their applications to legally inform you of things they do not want you to really notice).

We all have been in meetings where we heard splendid things. Perhaps we have even seen spectacular spiritual gifts displayed. But we have walked away with an ache in our hearts. Something was not totally as it should be.

Many years ago author Roxanne Brandt saw a vision of people ministering on a platform. They were terrific. The audience was receptive. But then she noticed Jesus. He was off in the corner, out of the spotlight. It broke her heart. Like the Greeks who came to Philip saying "We wish to see Jesus,"[6] there is a generation that will not be content with anyone or anything but Jesus. What else is there? *Who* else is there? Who do we have in heaven but Jesus? We will become increasingly dissatisfied with anyone else. As leaders our natural tendency is to steal the show. We love attention. As an audience, we have to admit we are loaves and fish people. We love the spectacular. We are naturally attracted to everything but Jesus. We need to be honest about it. The spotlight has always had a tendency to bounce off of Him and on to us.

Have you ever watched a soccer game on TV? As the camera pans the field and follows the ball, all of a sudden you become aware that there is an advertisement way off, on the backboard. Our presentations of Jesus are often like that. The close-up shots are all of us. Jesus is far off in the almost subliminal background. He's the commercial, not the main program. He is in the crowd shot, not the close-up. He is the assumed subject of the sentence, not the heart of the story.

Those involved in ministry can tell you how innocently it begins. As a child I grew up visiting the skidrow streets of Los Angeles several times a week. We dreamed of offering a clear, compelling message of Jesus' desire to save. We were passionate for the lost. Passion can be a beautiful thing, but it can also be dangerous. Slowly, almost imperceptibly, the focus easily gets bumped off Jesus the Shepherd, seeking the lost sheep, to us (by ourselves), scrambling down hillsides to bring back the wayward lamb. "Did you see the degree of that slope *I* went down?" The more lost sheep, the easier it is to start search and rescue operations on our own.

After a while we think we know just how to find them. We think we know what they need. We easily fall prey to an independence that says "Hey! I can do this. I am even good at this." We get judgmental because others are not out risking their necks to find lost sheep like we are. We start congratulating ourselves because we are willing to grab lambs out of the lion's mouth, and those other guys are at home, trying to decide which movie to watch. By the time we actually find the wayward lamb, we have lost sight of the Shepherd ourselves.

On skid row in the late 1960s, it was easy to get caught up in making sure we had enough bologna sandwiches to offer after the service. Our hearts may have been in the right place, but it was easy for our eyes to wander off Jesus and on to the need. That is purely a human tendency. That is why the Holy Spirit needs to continually remind us that it's all about Jesus, it's not about us.

JESUS, THE GREAT ASSUMPTION

Jesus is increasingly the assumed subject of the sentence, and less and less the heart of the story. You can attend many conferences today and hear much about spiritual technology and techniques—and very little about Jesus. We assume that our audience knows and loves Jesus. We speakers assume that we are Christ-centered and focused on His absolute sufficiency. But the sad reality is that the spotlight is generally peripheral to Jesus. Pick almost any conference at random and order any tape. Listen for Jesus. You will hear wonderful stories, stunning experiences that will fire your imagination. You will receive helpful principles and keen insights. You will possibly get a new perspective, and often an enlarged heart. You will usually find something helpful, but you rarely come away with more of Jesus. As Kathleen Norris observes, "The religious marketplace is full of spiritualities that can costume us in fancy dress."[7]

Recently I read a book by a popular author about the future of the Church and found Jesus assumed, but barely mentioned. Does the Church have a future apart from Jesus? I have led worship for Christian conferences where, in a three-day period, Jesus was only mentioned marginally. The first time it happened, I thought perhaps I simply was not paying enough attention. Maybe I just missed it. Then it happened again and again. Then I started watching for Him, anxious to find Him. I remember thirty years ago, Kathryn Kuhlman, a prominent healing evangelist, saying she had often gone to meetings and felt as if "They had taken away my Lord and I know not where they have laid Him." I was beginning to empathize.

One thing that gives me pleasure is to take black-and-white portraits of people I love. I remember reading a famous photographer's words: "You will know you are beginning to be a real photographer when you begin to miss the light." I do not know if I will ever be a *real* photographer, but in Christian circles, I am beginning to miss the Light. Jesus, the preeminent One, seems to be increasingly in the shadows, and few people seem to notice.

Pick up almost any Christian magazine, listen to a Christian radio or TV program, overhear the conversations of God's people and you will find Jesus, like Waldo, tucked away somewhere obscurely in the crowd. It does not even seem to matter what particular stream of the Body of Christ you are in: charismatic, liturgical, evangelical. You can find Jesus the assumed subject of the sentence almost anywhere in Christendom.

Recently I attended a meeting of highly visible national ministries. I left one breakfast gathering grieved to the bone. Jesus was loved by many taking part but He was not the center of the conversation. The meeting was full of very articulate, likeable, passionate people. But the center of the passion was not Jesus. The center of the passion in that particular gathering was purely political. As British author and theologian P. T. Forsythe says, "The chief plague and heresy of the hour . . . is that God tends to become the most fluid of all words. The prime certainty becomes the great haze.

He pervades but He does not purpose. He saturates all, but all does not center in Him."[8]

In the book of Revelation, the church at Ephesus is known for what they are against. They are against those who pretend to be apostles and really are not the Nicolaitans. The Ephesians have some great qualities. They have endurance, they have persevered in the face of overwhelming odds. The Ephesians cannot stomach the things God hates. They have a well-developed theology of againstness. I imagine the Ephesian believers might have had "No on Proposition 14" signs on their front lawns. They were diligent and informed on the issues. But God had a serious quarrel with them: The Ephesians had left their first love. Jesus was no longer their overriding passion.

Jesus may be *privately* the centerpiece of many spiritual leader's lives. Yet our *public* proclamation of Him grows increasingly faint. It is easy to observe Jesus becoming less and less the preeminent feature of our presentations. We are sadly known more for what we are against than for Who we are for. In many sectors of society, Christianity is thought to be akin to a front-range militia movement.

We tend to be more impressed with people and practices related to Him than we are of Him. Practices and perspectives of Christianity separate from the person of Christ become malignant. When principles *about* Him are isolated *from* Him, when we copy models and methods gotten from someone else's direction instead of our own, we have nothing to offer the world.

You cannot have a kingdom without a King. This King

does not hand out photocopies. This King is not just one ingredient of a formula. He *is* the formula. Karl Barth said that when he first became a Christian, he thought Jesus was the prophet of the kingdom. After many years he realized Jesus *was* the kingdom. Jesus is all we have been given by God to offer the world.

REVIVAL AS A DISTRACTION

I am privileged to co-lead a pastors' prayer summit in our region. Recently about sixty pastors gathered to spend a day together seeking God's face. Through years of honest but less-than-effective gatherings, we realized God was requiring us to come to Him without an agenda. We eventually realized that even *seeking revival* can become an agenda. We are easily distracted from Christ not only by emerging spiritual technologies, amazing people, and enthralling practices, but often by godly hopes as well.

As we began the prayer summit, Mark Patterson, a Presbyterian pastor who had just completed his doctoral thesis for a Ph.D. in systematic theology at King's College in London, shared what he'd learned while writing his dissertation on revival. Patterson said: "God has all these marvelous gifts He wants to give us. But whenever He does; we worship either the gift itself (the *practice*), the *place* where it came, or the *person* it came through. I have learned that people want revival more than they want Jesus."

We clearly live in a yeasty time, ripe for revival. Never before in history have so many people in so many nations

gone on extended fasts and prayed so fervently for revival.
Those prayers have not fallen to the ground. God's hand is
poised in our generation to do an astonishing thing on the
earth. But in our praying, what are we expecting? Do we picture a day when entire sports stadiums of people come to
Christ? When major network announcers show people being
raised from the dead on prime-time news? Do we envision a
long string of miracles done by ordinary everyday believers?
I do. But if that is all there is to revival, what do we have left
when the spectacular wanes? If revival were to come tomorrow, would we be so centered on Jesus that we could effectively mentor the millions God will bring to His Son?

As David Bryant says,

> From whatever angle we view it, . . . revival is fundamen-
> tally one thing: Revival is Christ . . . God can do nothing
> greater for His church than to reawaken us to the suffi-
> ciency, supremacy, and destiny of the Lord Jesus Christ . . .
> God does not possess anything for His people, now or for-
> ever, beyond who Christ is . . . Jesus exhausts for us all we
> can ever know about God.[9]

God's passion always has been and always will be Jesus.
Jesus is the entire heart of all God's stories.

Jesus is the heart of God's story in history. Jesus is the heart
of God's story in redemption. Jesus is the heart of God's story
in our present. Jesus is the heart of God's story in our future
destiny after the earth and heavens have been dissolved.

Many years ago author and missionary Roy Hession

conducted evangelistic campaigns. In his travels, he noticed that the health of the church had a lot to do with the harvest that was reaped. So he decided to spend one week simply ministering to Christians. He expected from this that Christians would become so healthy, so fired up, so full of prayer that his preaching to the unconverted the next week would be highly effective. But he did not see the anticipated results. He was puzzled. He sought God as to why his approach was not working. Then he realized he was encouraging people to use Jesus as a means to an end, not as the end itself. They were repenting and praying because they wanted to see a huge ingathering. Jesus was not the end of what they were seeking. He was simply the means to it. God would not honor His Son's being used, *even for revival.*

Roy Hession comments, "He Himself is Revival and the simple door to it . . . Is it not significant that when there is an experience of revival in lives, those revived do not talk about revival, but rather about Jesus?"[10] God's passion is the glory of His Son. As lovers of God, should our passion be any less? The holy ambition of God is for His Son to be loved, known, and obeyed in all the earth by all peoples. As David Bryant says: "God intends his Son to be at the center of everything—at the end of history and at every step along the way. He has no greater desire. In whatever He does his ultimate purpose is to sum up all heaven and earth under Jesus as Lord (see Ephesians 1:10). Every revival—including the final revival—is meant to accelerate, intensify, and expand this process."[11] Jesus is to be center and circumference of all our inquiry, energy, devotion, and interest. He is not merely first in our life but *to be* our very life. He is not an addendum, an interesting footnote to God's work in the world. He is the center of all life and endeavor.

PETER'S FOLLY

God is calling us to an undistracted passion for His Son. There are many dazzling things to distract us. The distractions are not necessarily evil. They are more like Moses and Elijah appearing with Jesus on the Mount of Transfiguration—interesting, even significant, but not where God desires our eyes to rest. Up on the Mount, Peter gasps with wonder at what he sees. Our open-mouth-change-feet apostle has yet another brilliant idea. Swept up in inconceivable awe at what is before his eyes, Peter wants to build three tabernacles. One for Moses, one for Elijah, and one for Jesus.

Poor Peter is clueless to the inappropriateness of his suggestion. Moses and Elijah are not *peers* with Jesus. He that is without equal—who cannot be compared to any other and for whom Moses and Elijah were born, stands transfigured there, burning radiantly with the light of a thousand suns. He who created worlds both visible and invisible—who holds all things together by the word of His power—He through whom all things consist is certainly not on *par* with these mighty prophets.

Moses *was* pretty impressive. He was the lawgiver, the one God used to institute the foundations of civilization.

God talked to him face-to-face as with a friend. He was called the meekest man on earth. His rod parted the Red Sea and struck rocks and caused water to gush out. His prayers produced an aboveground commissary of manna and quail—no refrigeration required.

Moses established the nation. His history with God could fill volumes. He was a songwriter, a military strategist, an intercessor, a miracle worker, a marriage and family counselor. Raising your eyebrows at Moses could carry significant risks. Moses' own sister, Miriam, developed leprosy due to criticizing him. The earth yawned in boredom, and swallowed up Korah and his complaining clan. Moses was not someone to trifle with. Moses was *certainly* worth commemorating.

And Elijah. Good heavens! Calling fire down from heaven on a soaked offering, shutting up the heavens from rain, and being boisterous with passion, zeal, and holy cockiness. The man who split rivers with his cloak, who raised the dead. *Of course* he deserves a tabernacle. Peter probably was surprised that Jesus was in such *amazing* company.

But before Peter could even get his three tabernacle suggestion out of his mouth, God thunders from heaven, *"This* is My beloved Son, hear *Him!"* Immediately Peter and John fall terrified on their faces. Jesus comes to them and says, "Do not be afraid." Immediately, only Jesus is in view.

Fast-forward the tape a couple of thousand years, and we are still like Peter. We want to put godly leaders on pedestals and build elaborate monuments to their anointings. We hang on every word they say as if it is God's own truth and idolize their miraculous signs. We know more details about the latest catastrophic prophecy than we do the character of Jesus. But God is fiercely intent on dissolving our distractions and having us see Jesus alone.

We will not be impoverished by our singularity of focus. Instead, we will be opening ourselves to the riches of God. When we have Jesus, we indeed have everything. All that God demands of us is met in Jesus. He is the supremely all-sufficient One, the first and last, the living One. Our greatest need, and God's greatest gift to us, is to awaken us to the sufficiency, supremacy, and destiny of the Lord Jesus Christ. We are called to an undistracted and lifelong preoccupation with Him.

Two

Jesus, the Heart of Our Devotional Life

---

*Christ is the central theme of Scripture. It is
the claim of the Bible itself . . . strung
out on the wash line of History.*[1]

—WALTER KAISER

*For if you believed Moses, you would believe Me; for
he wrote about Me.*[2]

—JESUS

My son slid close as I groggily read him the story of
Deborah and Jael. The narrative was humming along
when disaster crept in, tumbling my morning into a head-
spin. As Jael was about to hammer her tent peg through
Sisera's forehead, my extremely visual son said, "Mom,
Mom, Stop! I want to have a good day! This story is terrible!" He continued on in a distressed voice, saying what no
lover of God would ever want to hear. "Anyway Mom," he
said adamantly, "I like Jesus' personality better than God's.
Jesus was definitely more tender." I was stumped. Doom

slowly spiraled down on my soul like an airliner plunging straight into the ocean. Who would have guessed that reading Scripture would alienate my dear son from God? What should I do?

I rushed to explain. The words tumbled out of my mouth, like people's words do when they're nervous: "Jesus said, 'He who has seen Me has seen the Father.'"[3] I told him that without Jesus, we never would have understood God. Jesus was God made visible and knowable. Jesus was God wearing bones and skin. God was *in* Jesus reconciling the world to Himself.[4] I did my best, dredging up from memory every scripture I could think of at that hour of the morning. Joel eyed me with sleepy suspicion.

Obviously there would be no swift, casual answer. How can you adequately explain the Trinity early in the morning? I switched gears. Usually we try to turn whatever scripture we read into a prayer. As you can guess, I was hard-pressed to turn *that* particular passage into prayer. All I could manage was a pathetic, "Lord, raise up ordinary people who will deliver others from oppression with whatever they have in their hand."

That morning proved to me afresh that reading the Word sometimes is not all we think it should be. Often just starting takes more diligence than devotion. There are entire histories we do not understand, cultural traditions that strike us as peculiar, details that offend our delicate sensibilities. Some passages should have warning labels, "Not Suitable for Children's Bedtime (or Morning) Stories." Sometimes for me, reading almost anything else is easier.

More often than not, my devotional times in the Word are stale and disappointing. Missionary and author Roy Hession says: "Important as Bible study is, it can be strangely sterile and does not necessarily mean that the student is enjoying a transforming vision of the Lord Jesus Himself—though we shall never get very far without a patient and daily waiting on God over the Scriptures."[5] As a child, I gravitated to Scriptures piping hot with wrath. I swallowed hard as the words stung my eyes. I staggered to keep my equilibrium as a lover of God. Given my propensity for randomly opening to judgment scriptures, the fact that I spend my life writing and speaking about the tenderness of Jesus is a sheer miracle.

Jesus said, "Man shall not live by bread alone, but by every word that proceeds from the mouth of God."[6] David said, "Your word I have hidden in my heart, that I might not sin against You."[7] God wasn't kidding when He commanded, "This Book of the Law shall not depart from your mouth, but you shall meditate in it day and night, that you may observe to do according to all that is written in it. For then you will make your way prosperous, and then you will have good success."[8] Jesus said, "If you abide in Me, and My words abide in you, you will ask what you desire, and it shall be done for you."[9] And just in case we missed the totality of God's intent, Deuteronomy 6 commands us to talk about God's Word when we sit down and rise up, go to bed, and take our children for a hike. It is obvious that God intends Scripture to fill all our waking moments.

Saturating your mind with God's Word is not a suggestion. Biblical literacy is not just a specialty for the super-spiritual (whoever they might be). It is the meat and potatoes of the Christian's life. In our option-rich society it is hard to deal with the fact that God's commands are binding. The cosmos was made and held together by the Word of God. Everything we see, feel, and touch owes its existence to God's Word. Consequently, for us to speak contrary to God's Word is to intentionally unravel ourselves and our circumstances. To speak contrary to the Word of God is to deconstruct your own present and future.

Our need for the Word to occupy our minds completely is clear. The challenge is to develop a thought life that continually embraces the thoughts of God. Maybe we are stuck in the quagmire of habituated religious routine. We might use our devotional lives to impress God or others. We may be going to the Word for all the wrong reasons, much like the Pharisees Jesus rebuked when He said, "You search the Scriptures, for in them you think you have eternal life; and these are they which testify of Me."[10] (It is sobering to realize that Jesus was the sternest with those who knew the Scripture best.) Jesus made it unflappingly clear that all Scripture pointed in one direction, and that direction was Himself. One scholar goes so far as to say: "Once we truly grasp the message of the New Testament it is impossible to read the Old Testament again without seeing Christ on every page, in every story, foreshadowed or anticipated in every event and narrative."[11]

JESUS, OUR CENTER OF GRAVITY

Jesus is to be the heart, the center of gravity, of our devotional lives. If all Scripture points us to Jesus, how can we find Him? I can tell you, from experience, a million ways how *not* to. In my lifetime I have discovered just about every dead end. Here are a couple of my own well-worn red herrings. Do not approach God's Word like a school assignment from an exacting instructor waiting to grill you. Do not read the Word like an accountant reading the IRS tax code, looking for fine-print exemptions. It is scandalous to approach the Word of God like a refrigerator. "Hmmm, I wonder what I am in the mood for tonight. Maybe a little comfort . . . perhaps a little Psalm." God is not on a shelf with the dill pickles.

We often go to the Word with a host of unrealistic expectations. We want to be fed, to be nurtured, to walk away changed, to be transformed. We want to feel the brilliant, radiant presence of God. We want all the things that people say will happen if we read it. Of course exposing one's self to Scripture can certainly do all those things, and there is a long history of Scripture doing all that and more. But the problem is that we become the focus of our own pursuit. If we are the center and circumference of our devotional universe, the whole sum and substance of our own inquiry, our devotional reading and prayer will be flat, stale, and boring. And well they should be. We are stuffed with ourselves, "the self stuffed with self," as Walker Percy described boredom.[12] God cannot add anything to us because we are so full. As E. Stanley Jones says: "It is only empty hands that can grasp a whole Christ." [13]

Our devotional lives, our longings and yearnings for the transcendent, can become a distraction from the very One we are crying out for. In the novel *A Vow of Silence,* the novice mistress warns of this very thing.

"One of the hardest things you will ever have to do is cultivate detachment," she warns. "Detachment from all, save the things of the spirit. Detachment does not mean coldness or not caring, but it does mean the ability to set oneself apart, from all yearnings for transient things, all possessiveness, *even in the end from the very prayers and devotions so dear to our hearts.* These are only the finger pointing at the moon. Do not spend all your time looking at your finger." [14]

We are often so preoccupied with our thirst, our hunger, and our desire that we become our own engorged planet with a strong gravitational pull. All our devotion ends up being pulled back on us—our effort, our discipline, our perseverance, our disappointment in God's not meeting us just the way we expected. Author Roy Hession says:

> The inordinate seeking of inner spiritual experiences may thwart us finding our true goal, for if we make our purpose in life a quest for these things, we tend to become occupied with our personal experiences or lack of them. This produces the sad situation of hungry, dissatisfied Christians seeking out this speaker or that, hoping that he will be found to have the secret; or going to

this convention or conference, trying new formulas for blessing, seeking fresh experiences, and falling either into pride or despair . . . This leaves the Christian still self-centered. Occupied with himself and his experiences and it can lead to much mental anguish . . . Yet, all the time the One who alone can satisfy the heart is by our side, longing to be known and loved and proved."[15]

If we would approach the Word of God with deep humility—letting the text be what it is, and letting God say what He will from it, pointing us to Jesus, as He desires—we would begin to know wisdom. Our continual temptation is to turn our devotional lives into something important, something meaningful. We want it to be all about us, instead of all about Him. We want to control our experience with God, to "torque up a notch" His estimation of us. But we cannot control our love life with God. We are not the initiators. We cannot force God's love to manifest just because we are in the mood for it. We are entirely shipwrecked on the mercy and willingness of God to reveal Himself to us. We must begin at that point. Thomas Merton describes our plight:

In our desire to be "as gods"—a lasting deformity impressed in our nature by original sin—we seek what one might call a relative omnipotence; the power to have everything we want, to enjoy everything we desire, to demand that all our wishes be satisfied and that our will should never be frustrated or opposed. It is the need to have everyone else bow to our judgement and accept our declarations as law. It is the insatiable thirst for recognition. . .This claim to omnipotence, our deepest secret and our inmost shame is in fact the source of all our sorrows, all our unhappiness, and all dissatisfactions. It is a radical falsity . . . there are many acceptable and "sane" ways of indulging one's illusory claim to divine power. One can be, for example a proud and tyrannical parent—or a tearful and demanding martyr-parent. One can be a nagging perfectionist. One can be a clown or a daredevil. One can be rigidly conventional or blatantly unconventional. *One can even, alas, seek sanctity and religious perfection as an unconscious satisfaction of this deep and hidden impurity of soul which is man's pride.* [16]

Ouch! Merton summed up much of my devotional life in that last sentence. When we refuse to accept that we are accepted in our total unacceptability, we end up seeking to buy counterfeit righteousness on the black market, like Rolex watches in Hong Kong—genuine copies of a fake. We seek to impress God with our diligence, our devotion, our ability to persevere. And we probably can fool most people, but we soon find an aridity to our souls that is palpable.

A PERSON, NOT A PRINCIPLE

Part of our problem is we teach people to read the Word with their minds first and their hearts second. But God's Word is a definition of a person. God's Word is not *Basic Instructions Before Leaving Earth*. It is the revelation of a person in His fascinating multilayered personality. The Word of God is not a code of conduct; it is not a list of rules; it certainly is not a compilation of unconnected stories. It is a treasure map, and Jesus is the treasure. Clues to Him abound on every page.

Have you ever wondered how David came to fall so blazingly in love with God with just a few Scriptures at his disposal? (He may have only had the book of Job, the Pentateuch, and Joshua.) How was it that he had so much revelation about what God was like? David's intimacy in his devotional life was directly linked to his habits of meditation and contemplation. David said in Psalm 119:15-16: "I will meditate on Your precepts, and contemplate Your ways. I will delight myself in Your statutes; I will not forget Your word." David was granted revelation of the character and personality of God because He was looking for a person, not just a religious routine. David was a man after God's own heart, and you can read that sentence both ways. David followed hard after God's heart and was given much revelation. There are more than twenty-three specific prophecies in the Psalms about the Messiah to come, all of which Jesus precisely fulfilled.[17]

IT IS ALL ABOUT HIM

John Stott comments on the centrality of Christ in His teaching:

> The most striking feature of the teaching of Jesus is that He was constantly talking about Himself . . . This self-centeredness of the teaching of Jesus immediately sets Him apart from the other great religious teachers of the world.

They were self-effacing. He was self-advancing. They pointed men away from themselves saying, "That is the truth, so far as I perceive it; follow that." Jesus said, "I am the truth, follow me." The founder of none of the ethnic religions ever dared to say such a thing.[18]

If Jesus dared to be so central in His own proclamation, should we not allow Him to be central to our devotion? We might fear that, somehow, in centering on Jesus we might miss the Father. But in looking to Jesus, we need never fear we'll end up lopsided when it comes to the Trinity. Jesus said in John 17: "Glorify Your Son, that your Son also may glorify You" (v. 1). The Father is always glorified when Jesus is honored. The Holy Spirit points us to Jesus; the Father points us to Jesus; Jesus points us to the Father. The Trinity has within its makeup a holy reciprocity of honor. Being centered on Jesus is always safe, because the Father and the Holy Spirit are always giving Him preeminence. Jesus is destined by the Father to have preeminence in all things, world without end. That preeminence will never obscure the primacy of the Father or the place of the Holy Spirit, which Jesus says proceeds from the Father. It is simply the good pleasure of the Father to give Jesus the kingdom. It is the Father's good pleasure for us to rest our eyes and hope completely in His Son.

FRESH WAYS TO LOOK FOR JESUS

We are creatures prone to fall into weary ruts of religious habit. We need fresh new ways to savor the Word of God. I am always hungry for God's Word to point me to Jesus anew. One approach some of my Catholic brothers and sisters use is the practice of *Lectio Divina*, or holy reading. *Lectio Divina* has four parts: reading, meditation, prayer, and contemplation. It is not so much a program or process as it is a way. It really cannot be taught but simply entered into.

We read Scripture, humbly coming to it, letting it be what it is. We marinade that Scripture in our minds, ruminating on it as a cow chews its cud, thinking through all the possibilities. Then, we turn that Scripture into prayer asking God to pray through us His intent, His holy ambition. Then we contemplate—we allow ourselves to be silently bathed in the love of God as revealed in the Scripture. In *Lectio Divina* we are not in a hurry. The object is not to see how much Scripture we can consume, but how much God's Words can consume us. When Bonhoeffer founded the seminary at Finkenwalde in Germany, everyone there practiced a daily half-hour of silent meditation on Scripture. In fact, Bonhoeffer recommended spending a whole week on a single text.[19]

Another approach many people find helpful is keeping a Scripture journal. My friend, author and Bible teacher Joy Dawson, suggests writing out whole sections of the Word. Begin to create your own personal concordance on the character and personality of God. She says,

> The main purpose in having the Bible is not that we may study its historical backgrounds, the lives of the people recorded in it, or its Hebrew or Greek. Nor is it that we

may memorize it or gain a lot of general knowledge about it. Rather, the main purpose in having the Bible is that we may seek to understand the *Author of the Book and live in intimate friendship with Him.*

She goes on to say, "One ounce of meditation is worth a ton of memorization, as important as that is. Because meditation produces revelation. And revelation motivates us to worship Him and obey Him."[20] We can easily fall into the trap of trying to master the contents of the Bible, but it is not about the "what," or the "where," or the "when." It is always and singularly about the Who. Who is Jesus, what is His personality, what is His character, what can I know of Him? Our devotional life will only be soul nourishing and satisfying as it leads us to Jesus.

When the apostle John was on Patmos, he was given a vision of heaven. The Lord appeared to him and said, "I am the Alpha and the Omega, the First and the Last,' and 'What you see, write . . ."[21] Many of my friends find keeping a journal of the clues they find about Jesus helps them stay focused and provides them with a trail of discovery. They forge a secret history with God through their written observations.

The Bible is a prayer book, first and foremost. You can be sure that you are never praying amiss, when you turn Scripture into prayer. Try taking a chapter like John 15 and pray it verse by verse. I always ask my son when he reads to turn the Scripture into prayer; even if it is a list of measurements for the temple, you can thank God that

He is very specific about things. And Jesus is the consummate specificity of God. The Holy Spirit longs to reveal Jesus to you as you learn the discipline of turning all Scripture into prayer.

Another creative approach many have found helpful is to turn your devotion into spontaneous singing. You might sound more like Bob Dylan than Andrea Bochelli, but just try singing a simple, spontaneous tune from Scripture. Borrow a folk melody if you like. This morning I read the passage in Hosea where God describes Himself with a metaphor from nature: "I am like a green cypress tree; your fruit is found in Me."[22] Now there's a verse you can sing to any tune (even "Three Blind Mice")! You do not need a passage to rhyme. Just start singing and see what happens. I promise you it will deepen your memory of the Word. When we look for Jesus in that passage, we remember John 15 in which Jesus, using the metaphor of a vine instead of a tree, says the exact same thing.

Creatologist/futurist/seminary president/author Leonard Sweet buys a new Bible each year with the express purpose of writing in it so that he can eventually give it to one of his children. What a splendid way to impart to our children (or our grandchildren) a lineage of love for God's Word. Can you imagine the impact of receiving a Bible from a loving parent, knowing that some of the tearstains on the pages landed there because someone was weeping out loud for love for you?

I started this chapter telling you of my disastrous encounter reading to my son the story of Jael hammering the tent peg through Sissera's temple. I started thinking, *If this chapter is true, there will be some way that dreadful, bloody story points to Jesus.* Where else in Scripture does something sharp pierce someone and the result is freedom from the oppressor? Where is the prophecy that a woman will crush the head of the enemy? Could it be that Jael's tent peg, and the nails that went into Jesus, are connected metaphorically? Could it be that just as a tent peg killed an oppressor of Israel, so the nails that pierced Jesus resulted in the death of the power of oppression forever? Could every story really point to Jesus?

The Holy Spirit has no greater delight than to help us find Jesus in every story, on every page, in every line. Jesus said of the Holy Spirit, who comes from the Father, "He will glorify Me, for He will take of what is Mine and declare it to you."[23] When we embrace the entrance of the Word of God into our thought lives, it will always lead us to Jesus. He is God's final and ultimate Word. He is the complete adequacy and sufficiency for all that God requires of us. Our greatest need is, always and constantly, more revelation of Him.

Three

Jesus, the Heart of Our Worship

For all the military metaphors in the Old Testament, the command that Israel receives most often is sing.[1]

—KATHLEEN NORRIS

There were more creative people per square inch than I thought possible in a local congregation. Our church was teeming with artists of all types: visual; musical; you name it, we had it. Unknown to us at the time, we were also teeming with serious problems. In fact, our problems were so systemic that they eventually caused the church's demise. After years of reflection, I think a postmortem might include a list of several spiritual malignancies.

We burned with passionate zeal for God. Our hearts ached to offer to the Lord something worthy of His name. We were genuine lovers of God and ran hot with desire to bring Him pleasure. We were willing to sacrifice anything. If it took being "green berets for Jesus," that was precisely what we would be. It was an incredible privilege for me to be one of several worship leaders in this creative group of wholehearted friends.

Our major message and emphasis was worship. We poured everything into it. Jesus was our great obsession. We panted after Him, gave Him our all. We were thoroughly educated on worship, and yet, as is often the case, we were clueless about the state of our own hearts. We gradually, inch by inch, fell down the slippery slope of worshiping worship. We fell prey to a subtle haughtiness, an insidious spiritual pride, that *our* theology of worship was more correct, more cutting edge. *We* were willing to lay down our lives more than other congregations. We longed to see the arts restored to worship. We were convinced the Lamb was worthy of absolutely everything that could be offered to Him; and we would be the ones who gave it, no matter what the cost. Never mind if others were stuck in the mire of tradition; we were willing.

Our pastor (who has since gone to be with the Lord) had an enormous heart for God. He would literally weep when watching the Olympics or other sporting events, longing to give his all for God and finish well. God had used him mightily in revival. As a result he was esteemed with high reverence in one particular region of the world. The exploits God had accomplished through him had been written up in *Life* magazine and other major news outlets.

He was a well-educated man in the process of completing his second doctorate. We were a well-fed congregation. Attending our services was a graduate-level experience in the Word. Major speakers in the Christian world would hear our pastor and say they had never heard anything so deep. Here was a man who passionately loved God with his entire being.

We exported our understanding of worship to many nations. Several of the choruses that were written in our church are still being sung all over the world. My husband and I were on a team that taught worship throughout Europe. I led one team to do the first worship symposium for pastors in the Philippines. People were hungry and receptive.

We knew we had discovered what the rest of the Body of Christ was missing. Nothing seemed impossible to us. To give you a hint of our earnestness (and lack of boundaries), one Christmas, with only two weeks' preparation, we put on a ballet to Handel's *Messiah* at the local community college auditorium.

Sadly, imperceptibly at first, the spotlight gradually slipped away from Jesus. We moved incrementally from the simplicity of devotion to Christ to trying harder and harder to strive for the mastery. Someone laughingly made the comment that we expected Jesus to appear on the overhead. That statement was not far from true. I remember being hesitant to take vacations, thinking that we might be out of town when God came and accepted our offering by fire. We began to mercilessly critique ourselves. We were positive we could do it better for God *if we just tried harder.* We fell prey to a corrosive self-centered evaluation of ourselves before the presence of God.

If anyone had pointed out that we were defecting from the simplicity of devotion to Christ, we would have been insulted. "But we are doing all this stuff for Him!" we would have replied. "It's because He's so worthy!" We would have shaken our heads, shocked that our brothers and sisters did not understand. They just did not grasp the biblical precedents of worship. They were content to just sit in pews and sing three hymns. We, on the other hand, would give God our all.

C. S. Lewis observes that many times our worship can turn into smugness. "We are appalled that others can only see gray when we are delicately observing such subtle nuances of pearl, dove, and silver."[2] We were enjoying the subtle nuances of Greek and Hebrew roots, a sweeping understanding of Hebraic thought. We were definitely in the know.

Like an adopted child who finally finds his birth parents, we were part gnostic and did not know it. Eugene Peterson describes how gnostics think:

> The gnostic line is quite convincing when we first come across it. There is an ascetical earnestness and mystical intensity that catches our attention. Because these people seem to be so deeply concerned about the inner life and to know so much more than anyone else about the graduate levels of spirituality, we are attracted and want to know more. But beware the gnostics: it is difficult to dislike them, harder still to label them, for the forms are protean. A great deal of what they say and do is beautiful. But there are two elements that through their influence insinuate themselves into the prayer of faith. These elements are

corrosive and can be fatal: contempt for the material and lust for the secretive. "Gnosticism" says Virginia Stem Owens, "is still the biggest lie of all. Gnostics are proto-typical insiders. They think that access to the Eternal is by password and that they know the password."[3]

Our contempt of the material world and scrupulosity took the form of a constant laying aside the demands of the integrity of common life. We were in services con-stantly. This left little time for developing friendships with those who did not know God. It also left little time for the hallowedness of the ordinary—like laundry or spending the night just goofing off with your kids or getting to know your neighbors.

Our lust was for the presence of God. It was a greedy lust. We had a serious addiction for more. If we felt God's presence tangibly in one service, well, the next service bet-ter top that. It was like having a rating scale for intimate times with your spouse. We began to critique sunsets. We went over everything we did with a fine-tooth comb for the express purpose of making it better.

We forgot that, as Richard Foster says, "We can never master that which the objective *is to be* mastered."[4] We complicated the simplicity of worship through our efforts to master it. We did think that "access to the Eternal [was] by password," and that we knew that password. We believed that password was *worship,* and we gave it our all. Early on, we did have some incredible experiences in the presence of Jesus. But those experiences only confirmed our error-laced theology. The experiences did not lead us into greater dependency on Jesus, but rather they confirmed for us that worship was the key to Jesus. That was the heresy.

BEWARE A RELIGIOUS SPIRIT

Any time we embrace anything other than Jesus as the key to God's heart, we open ourselves to the malignant deformation of a religious spirit. A religious spirit always accents what we do or what we know, instead of Whose we are and Who we know. A religious spirit always holds up the mirror before our own faces, not before the face of Jesus. Its focus is inward—ourselves, our performance of religious routine, our spiritual resume. In contrast, the Holy Spirit (who does not possess a shred of religion) always points us to Jesus. When we believe the lie that we can please God through effort, we negate the entire purpose of the cross. We become an enemy of all that God intends for us through His Son.

This is why Jesus often blasted the self-righteousness, all the while being tender and compassionate with rank-and-file sinners. Jesus had nothing but scathing, boiling words for the religious hierarchy. "But woe to you, scribes and Pharisees, hypocrites! For you shut up the kingdom of heaven against men; for you neither go in yourselves, nor do you allow those who are entering to go in."[5] Religion that bars the door and only lets the initiated into the deeper things of God, is the first whiff of heresy. There are no keys, no passwords, no hidden knowledge that gets you entrance to Jesus. He is the door. He, Himself, is the key. He said "The one who comes to Me I will by no means cast out."[6]

A religious spirit is puffed and stuffed with pride, and pride always divides. Love, on the other hand, always includes. Love always sets another place at the table, whereas pride prefers to dine alone, or at least in very select company. Pride always applauds self, while love applauds others. If there is any modicum of spiritual pride in you, show it the door immediately lest it ruin your whole house.

Our church paid dearly for our theological error. It closed, leaving a mixed legacy. Some have pleasant memories. But for many the wounds go deep and color perceptions, even now, of authentic worship. A few who attended, while remaining lovers of God, no longer attend church anywhere. For me personally, because of my own sin, many years passed before I felt comfortable leading worship again.

BACK TO THE FUTURE

We often need to begin at the end to understand this present moment. God intends to have His Son occupy the center stage of history. As Lord of history He has given Jesus the name that is above every name. He occupies the place that is above every place. It is to Him that every knee bows and every tongue confesses His lordship.

For by Him all things were created that are in heaven and that are on earth, visible and invisible, whether thrones or

dominions or principalities or powers. All things were created through Him and for Him. And He is before all
things, and in Him all things consist . . . that in all things
He may have the preeminence.[7]

As John sees the Lamb in the book of Revelation, He is the
central figure of worship. He is the One standing in the
midst of the lampstand, "eyes pouring fire-blaze . . . His
face a perigee Sun." John faints dead away, and Jesus picks
him up. "Do not fear, I am First, I am Last, I'm Alive. I
died, but I came to life and my life is forever. See these keys
in my hand?"[8] True worship centers on Jesus. It is not
about us. It is about Him. It has *always* been about Him
and nothing else. It is not about the arts, culture, tradition.
It is not about style. It is not about musical preference.
(Most music wars in the church are simply a matter of
preference, rarely substance). Worship is not even about
music, period. It's not about anything but *Him.*

JESUS, THE GLORY OF THE FATHER

Jesus *is* the glory of the Father. In John 17 Jesus prays that
we may be with Him to *see* His glory. When Moses
pleaded with God to see His glory, God answered and said
that He would allow His goodness to pass before Moses.
Unlike Moses, we ask to see many things: more anointing,
more miracles, more provision, more influence. But
Moses asked to see God's glory. He wanted to know God's
character and ways. God's glory is His goodness, and His
goodness is completely summed up in Jesus Christ.

When Moses saw God's glory pass before him, he heard God say, "The LORD, the LORD God, merciful and gracious, longsuffering, and abounding in goodness and truth, keeping mercy for thousands, forgiving iniquity and transgression and sin . . ."[9] God's glory is simply a description of His character. And God's character is perfectly presented in the person of Jesus. Moses' prayer to see God's glory could be one of the reasons that Jesus is seen with Moses and Elijah on the Mount of Transfiguration. Could it be that God allowed Moses to come back and see His glory perfectly demonstrated in His Son?

In his biography of Martin Luther, D'Augigne describes how Luther wanted to know God. "He wished to penetrate into the secret councils of God, to unveil His mysteries, to see the invisible and to comprehend the incomprehensible." His teacher checked him. He told him not to presume to fathom the hidden God but to confine himself to what He has shown us in Jesus Christ. "In Him, God has said, you will find what I am and what I require. Nowhere else neither in heaven nor in the earth will you discover it."[10] In Jesus the full character of God is perfectly revealed.

Jesus is the center of our worship because He is the perfect revelation of God. "For it pleased the Father that in Him all the fullness should dwell."[11] No aspect of God was left out. In Jesus there is no deficiency in God's greatness, His power, His holiness. When we worship Jesus, we are worshiping the character and personality of God fully expressed in His Son.

Worship is, as John Piper says,

feeling, thinking, speaking, and acting in a way that magnifies the infinite beauty and greatness of Christ. Not the way a magnifying glass magnifies, but the way a telescope magnifies. Microscopes move the appearance of size away from reality. Telescopes move the appearance of size toward reality. So worship displays Christ the way He really is—infinitely beautiful and infinitely great.[12]

True worship consists of our bringing who we actually are *to who He actually is*, coming to Him with our everyday lives. Our moment-by-moment, still-need-to-brush-my-teeth, shave-my-face, take-the-dog-for-a-walk, lives. Worship is not a performance, a spectacle, an entertainment show for deity.

> Your worship must engage your spirit in the
> pursuit of truth. That's the kind of people the
> Father is out looking for: those who are
> simply and honestly themselves before him
> in their worship. God is sheer being itself—
> Spirit. Those who worship him must do it
> out of their very being, their spirits, their
> true selves, in adoration. (John 4:24 THE MESSAGE)

Worship is bringing your true self to the true self of the Holy One. No pretense, no showiness, no putting on a costume. Sometimes we think we need to bury our messy, frustrated selves in order to truly worship. When we do, we create fake selves that methodically click out religious routine. God is not fooled. He does not receive fake worship for anything other than what it is. Isaiah sobbed, "These people draw near with their mouths and honor Me with their lips, but have removed their hearts far from Me, and their fear toward Me is taught by the commandment of men."[13]

Look at the best worship literature in history, the Psalms. David's worship is freighted with complaints; he was frighteningly honest with God. "Why do you cast me off? Why do I go mourning because of the oppression of the enemy?"[14] Honesty is potent worship. Sometimes in a worship service, I realize that God would prefer to hear what I am really thinking than to see me simply put myself on automatic pilot. How many times have I sung, "Lord I love you," when I was really thinking about how much I'd really rather be somewhere else? Do I really think God will not notice?

WORSHIP IS NOT CONFINED TO MUSIC

Music is just one planet in a whole universe of possible responses to the Wonderful One. Worship is not merely an emotional gift. We worship with our wills. We worship with our minds. We worship with our imaginations. We worship when we obey God at great cost. I have a friend who loves to surf, who never could picture herself anywhere in the world but near an ocean. And God called her to a country as far away from the ocean as you can get. Her life is one continual act of bowing low in worship.

Jesus said, "If you love Me, keep My commandments."[15] Loving God is simply obeying Him.

Romans 12 commands us to present our bodies as a living sacrifice, holy, acceptable to God, which is our reasonable worship. Presenting God with our lives, our hopes, our desires, presenting Him with our total self, warts and all, is worship. Every waking moment can be pure worship as we continually turn our hearts toward Jesus.

When we think of worship in a purely musical sense, we unconsciously create a spiritual elite. Recently a man was asked how it was that he went into a dump and planted churches and created leadership that planted more churches in a very short amount of time. Others at that same location had taken years to plant churches and never produced leaders that planted other works. They said there just was not any leadership material in their converts. And yet this man had marvelous results. What was his secret? He answered that he never did anything that a one-week-old Christian could not do. He never prayed like he normally prays, preached like he normally preached, or worshiped like he normally worshiped. He especially did not bring in worship bands, because people might have thought they had to have a lot of talent to worship. He limited himself to doing what any one-week-old Christian could do. When new converts saw the simplicity of his preaching and his worship, they knew they could easily do what he did. And so planting new churches and raising up new leaders was normal.

There was nothing complicated; all that they saw was

simple devotion to Christ. If they had seen highly talented professional worship leaders, they would have thought, "We'd better leave all that worship stuff to the professionals." It is always easier to be a spectator than a participant. Even if you are tone deaf, you can be a consummate worshiper of Jesus. Nourish your soul with high thoughts of Him. Learn to cultivate gratitude for the slightest things. My mom often thanks God for even a glass of water. Considering the drought in many places on the earth, that is not a bad idea. Everything you look at can prompt you to worship.

If music is our sole criterion for defining worship, it is not only limiting, it can slowly become the object of our worship. Of course, I am not recommending that we do away with music. I am a worship leader and a songwriter. But we need to be careful that music does not become the thing that defines our devotion. Matt Redman, a gifted worship leader/songwriter from England encountered this occupational hazard in a congregation he serves. Matt leads worship for Soul Survivor, a growing youth congregation near London, England.

Matt's pastor, Mike Pilavachi, explains:

I noticed that although we were singing the songs, our hearts were far from Him . . . we had become connoisseurs of worship instead of participants. In our hearts we were giving the worship marks [on a scale] of ten: 'Not that song again,' 'I cannot hear the bass,' 'I like the way she sings . . .' We had made the band the performers of worship and ourselves the audience. We had forgotten that we are all the performers of worship and that God is the audience. We had forgotten that sacrifice is central to biblical worship. We needed to take drastic action. We banned the band. We sacked Redman! Then we sat around in circles and said that if no one brought a sacrifice of praise, we would spend the meeting in silence. At the beginning, we virtually did! It was a very painful process. We were learning again not to rely on the music. After a while we began to have some very sweet times of worship.

We began to bring our prayers, our readings, our prophecies, our thanksgiving, our praises, and our songs. Someone would start a song a cappella and we would all join in. We were not having church; we were once again meeting with God. With all the comforts stripped away we worshiped from the heart. After we learnt our lesson, we brought the band back. Matt wrote this song out of our experience.[16]

> *When the music fades,*
> *All is stripped away,*
> *And I simply come.*
> *Longing just to bring*
> *Something that's of worth*
> *That will bless Your heart.*
> *I'll bring You more than a song.*
> *For a song in itself is not what*
> *You have required.*
> *You search much deeper within,*

Through the way things appear;
You're looking into my heart.
I am coming back to the heart of worship,
And it's all about You,
All about You, Jesus.
I am sorry Lord for the thing I have made it.
When it's all about You.
All about You, Jesus.
King of endless worth
No one could express
How much You deserve.
Though I am weak and poor
All I have is Yours,
Every single breath.[17]

MATT REDMAN © 1997

KINGSWAY'S THANKYOU MUSIC

Four

Jesus, the Heart of Our Thought Life

If we will fill our souls with the written gospel, we will refuse to devote our mental space and energy to the fruitless, even stupefying and degrading stuff that clamors for our attention.[1]

—DALLAS WILLARD

Gird up the loins of your mind, be sober, and rest your hope fully upon the grace that is to be brought to you at the revelation of Jesus Christ.[2]

—PETER

Be on guard if you ever come to our house. My son and I ensnare the unsuspecting in a mean game called Mind Occupation. It is a simple way to momentarily sculpt a person's thought life. The goal is to start a song that will lodge in the person's brain for hours. The victim retaliates by coming up with a song so powerful that it not only eradicates your song from their brains but lodges their song firmly in yours. Joel and I have garnered a list of never fails–tunes for the occasion. One we have found particularly useful is "Yankee Doodle." (Go ahead; try not to hear it!)

If the only people interfering with your thought life are Joel and me, you are relatively safe. Of course, every business on the planet will pay handsomely to insert their little jingle in your mind. There are plenty of vain philosophies clamoring for rental space as well—not to mention a certain adversary, who prizes your mind as prime real estate and will pay any going rate. Author and city-taking strategist Ed Silvoso wisely observes that the greatest strongholds are between your ears. The richest real estate in the world is definitely your mind, and there is no shortage of people waiting in line to lodge there.

When I was young and the space race was at the top of our national agenda, I remember people saying, "Whoever controls space controls earth." While that may be true, the stronger fact is that whoever controls the space between your ears controls you. Did you ever sing the little song "Oh, Be Careful Little Ears What You Hear"? As a child I remember my mom having a cast iron door stopper made out of three monkeys. One monkey had his hands over his eyes; one had his hands over his ears; and one had his hand over his lips. They were the see-no-evil-hear-no-evil-speak-no-evil monkeys, and I remember them with great fondness. I have not seen them for years. I hope they make a comeback. We need to be reminded often of the truth. We must be guarded gatekeepers of what we take in visually and audibly, and of what we say. We are only as whole as our thought life is pure.

The things you allow your mind to see and savor, and the things you listen to, form who you are and who you become. Watching little children play can tell you in five minutes what they watch and what they listen to. You might think visual images and story lines do not affect you, that they just roll right off. One friend said to me, "Shoot, I watched cowboy westerns all my growing up years, and it did not affect me a bit." But if image and sound are so ineffectual, why are advertisers willing to spend billions on advertising? Are they wasting their money? They do not think so.

The Scripture is shot through with injunctions about the seriousness of what we allow into our thought life. David said "I will set nothing wicked before my eyes."[3] Solomon says, "As he thinks in his heart, so is he."[4] Jesus says a startling thing about eyes in Mark 9:47. He says to pluck out your right eye if it offends. Not exactly a seeker-sensitive sentence to be sure. (Proving once again that Jesus would probably not be invited back as a speaker for most spiritual life conferences.) He even said that it is better to lose a foot than to leapfrog into hellfire with both feet.

MINDKEEPERS AS GATEKEEPERS

In days past gatekeepers played a strategic role in the safety of a city. The gatekeepers determined who got in and who got out. They determined who looked suspicious and who was trustworthy. Gatekeepers kept foreign invaders from ransacking the city. If you knew an army was heading your direction, your first priority was to close your gates. As a gatekeeper it was never a good idea to fall asleep in the middle of your watch. You might wake up and find yourself in another country, gatekeeping a jail cell from the inside out. The Chinese imagined that if they built an enormous wall around their country, it would prevent marauding invaders. Yet, barely was the Great Wall of China finished when the Chinese had already been invaded three times. The invaders never even threw a rope over the wall. They did not go over it or under it. They simply went through the gate. All they had to do was bribe the gatekeeper.

Our eyes, our ears, our imaginations, and our mouths are our gates. The enemy has no access to us apart from those four gates. This is why the enemy invests so much in music, movies, video games, and entertainment. I believe much of our coldness and indifference to Jesus is due to sleeping on the job as gatekeepers of our own and our childrens' inner lands. Like the gatekeeper on the Great Wall, we have allowed ourselves to be bribed by exhaustion, entertainment, and apathy.

Being a gatekeeper is no easy task. It requires diligence at every entrance, at every moment. Often we are guilty of selective gatekeeping. Some people guard carefully what they see and hear, but they ignore what goes out of their mouths. Others keep a tight reign on their tongue, yet give a free pass to anything coming through their eyes. Extreme diligence is required all along the wall, at every gate. We must not allow ourselves to be bribed by our fear of others' opinions. Our family recently went out with some friends to a movie that looked promising. Five minutes into the movie I realized it was not appropriate for adults or children. Unfortunately I was so afraid of being perceived as "holier than thou" that I did not walk out. I was embarrassed that I crumbled under peer pressure. (Some theaters will refund your money if you leave during the first fifteen minutes.)

Sloppy gatekeeping welcomes the enemy's entrance. Do we watch what we watch? Do we scrutinize what we listen to? Do we think entertainment is harmless? Are we persevering and vigilant in keeping a watchful guard over every entrance? Or do we collapse before the smooth god of comfort: "Oh, I am terribly tired tonight. I think I'll just veg out in front of the television." The truest clues to who we actually are are contained in our speech and thought life. Speech reveals the inward man. It is the most direct clue to someone's personality. Your thought life is you.

David, for most of his life, was a careful gatekeeper of his soul. He meditated day and night on the Word of God. He let his thoughts marinate in the thick wisdom of God. God's thoughts were his delight, his joy. Because David, like Job, esteemed God's Words more than his necessary food, he had insight into the ways of God. David prayed "Let the words of my mouth and the meditation of my heart be acceptable in Your sight."[5] David's exemplary thought life alerts us, however, to a very real danger. Guarding your gates yesterday is no protection against today's advancing army.

David, though steeped in God's thoughts, ends up God's poster-child for grace. Not only was he the sweet psalmist of Israel, he was an adulterer, a murderer, and a dismally poor father as well. David's tragedy came from letting his thought life run wild. His life proves to us that guarding our gates is never a one-act play. No matter how much we have been saturated with the Word in the past, we must keep a present diligence. David's adulterous relationship with Bathsheba and his murder of her husband happened when he let his guard down and let his thoughts wander.

David's unchecked thought life came at a point of tiredness. He was tired of battle (it was at the time when kings normally go to battle). We are most vulnerable when we are most tired. David looks where he should not look, desires what he should not have, and Bathsheba ends up with a baby in her womb. Sin always conceives something. David tries to cover his sin by ordering her husband home from the war. Her husband, conscious of his fellow soldiers, refuses to go home and lay with her. At every turn God thwarts David's attempts to hide his sin. His secret unraveling, David in desperation finally murders her husband.

The prophet Nathan comes with a simple story and the convicting finger of the Holy Spirit, and David repents. He pays a dear price for his sin. His secret becomes common knowledge to all succeeding generations, he gives the enemies of God occasion to blaspheme, he watches helplessly while his child dies. All because he did not guard his eye gate.

Your eyes, your ears, your imagination, and your soul need to be guarded with all diligence. Proverbs 4:23 says

"Keep your heart with all diligence, for out of it spring the issues of life." In the Hebrew that verse could read, "Be a watchman of your inner man." Whatever we think about, we become. We have the injunction in Philippians 4:8: "Whatever things are true, whatever things are noble, whatever things are just, whatever things are pure, whatever things are lovely, whatever things are of good report, if there is any virtue and if there is anything praiseworthy—meditate on these things."

PRESCRIPTION FOR MENTAL HEALTH

Far from being some mystical ideal, I think Paul is giving us a marvelous prescription for mental health. Who else is pure, lovely, and noble but Jesus? When we fix our minds on Him, we find our thought life increasingly bathed in peace. God promises to keep us in perfect peace when our minds are stayed on Him.[6] Literacy advocate Frank Laubach had a game with minutes, where he encouraged everyone he could to try to think about Jesus at least once every minute of the day. He recorded his successes in a little book entitled *A Game with Minutes*. Instead of finding it bothersome, he found it exhilarating to keep his mind on Jesus.

BOUNTY HUNTERS OF
OUR THOUGHT LIFE

Paul uses curious language when he exhorts us to take every thought captive to the obedience of Christ.[7] Can you picture someone hunting through your inner thought life, intent on seizing every thought for a catch-and-release program? Can you see that same hunter holding a thought up to the light of God's revealed Word to see how it sizes up, much like a fisherman measuring a fish to see if he can keep it? Declare open season on your thought life and you will discover that you are keeping many destructive thoughts that are like fish infested with worms.

If you are anything like me, you have a familiar groove of thought, a network of inner voices that cooperate to steal your hope. The thoughts may pose as questions, but really are snares in disguise. Thoughts such as *What difference is this really going to make?* pose as legitimate questions. They are instead sharpened arrows fashioned to bleed our peace. Recently I was putting together a county wide prayer event, thinking to myself, *Will this really make a difference?* You would think I would recognize immediately that particular thought needed to be captured and brought into the obedience of Christ. After all, God promises that the fervent prayer of a righteous man accomplishes much. Obviously my thought was in direct contradiction to the Word. We know God gets smile wrinkles when His people seek Him. But I was slow to capture that thought and subject it to the truth of Christ. I mulled it over in my mind and let my spirit fatally stew for most of the morning. The seeming futility of having invested nine years in gathering people for prayer overwhelmed and disheartened me.

I have a friend who loves to say, "Do not let your mind wander. It's too little to be out on its own." My mind was loose and wreaking havoc with my hope. Your thought life left unchecked will eventually wreak ruin on your life. An undisciplined thought life will seek to abort the destiny of God for your life.

When Jesus is the heart of our thought life, we allow His mind, His thoughts, His prayers, and His desires to fill our waking moments. Any thought contrary to the true character and personality of Jesus is malignant and needs to be quickly removed. Inner thoughts that disparage His character fester like maggots in your soul. Proverbs 16:3 says: "Commit your works to the Lord and your thoughts will be established." It is not as difficult as you might at first imagine.

It Needs to Be Intentional

Making Jesus the heart of our thought life requires intentionality. We do not just wake up some morning and find our minds fixed on Jesus. God does not sprinkle magic focusing dust on us while we are asleep. Becoming a person occupied 24/7 by Jesus, the Maker of our minds, will require vigilance and hard choices. We will need to adopt a new carefulness, a new attentiveness to our exposure. Author Dallas Willard says: "The key to loving God is to see Jesus, to hold him before the mind with as much fullness and clarity as possible."[8]

The Bible is explicit in its demands about what we feed our inner man. Before you activate your legalism shield, hear me out. I do not mean to be prescriptive in any way.

But we often have differing weights and measures about what we visually ingest. I am not Victorian, and I am not a prude. I happen to think sex is one of God's marvelous ideas. But I do not know anyone who would allow two strangers to openly make love in their front room in front of everyone, and yet almost no one I know turns it off if it's on television. Is there really a difference? What we would never allow in real life, we often allow if it's a movie. Some times we think we need to watch certain things to keep culturally relevant. But we do not have to float through a sewer in a glass-bottom boat to get a handle on the ramifications of sin.

Know Your Own Vulnerability

Our gatekeeping duties are not limited to pure visual image. We need to be vigilant about what we read and what we hear. We each have different vulnerabilities. I find certain kinds of theological literature completely debilitating; much of it excites my inherent agnosticism and propels me away from Jesus. For others; their vulnerabilities run toward intellectualism; for them to read certain books is as toxic as going to an Internet pornography site.

Feast on What Is Good

Discipline your eyes; reign in your ears. Do not just fast from the impure; feast on what is good. Realize God is not out to frustrate and seriously hamper your joy. When He says "No," it's for the same reason I tell my son "no" about a candy bar. I know what Joel does not. I am fixing his favorite dessert for dinner, mud pie. Because God is fixing up something beyond anything we can imagine, He does not want us to spoil our appetite. God's restrictions allow room for His delights. He says do not set something vile before your eyes, because I do not want your appetite satiated with less than beauty and wonder and everything good. G.K. Chesterson said the "chief purpose for rules is to let everything *good* run wild."

God wants us to feast on what nourishes our soul. He's not a bore, a dud, a stick-in-the-mud God. Far from it. He has more capacity for pleasure than you ever thought of having. David says, "In Your presence is fullness of joy; At Your right hand are pleasures forevermore."[9] God says He'll make us abundantly satisfied and cause us to drink of the rivers of His pleasures.[10] God does not want to end your enjoyment; He intends to enlarge and enhance it. Jesus invites us to feast on wonder. Consummate wonderer, author Annie Dillard, observes, "The world is fairly studded and strewn with unwrapped gifts and free surprises . . . cast broadside from a generous hand."[11] There are several lifetimes of wonder right in your own backyard. Our backyard is a mountain, and we have an amazing assortment of birds who call it home. Each of them has a very distinctive voice. We have a large owl who makes certain peculiar noises when he has a tasty meal within range. Some nights he sounds as if he's going to come in our bedroom window and sleep with us. Red-tailed hawks play aerial sentinel over our canyons. I wonder what they think about. One bird sounds like a Kalahari Bushman speaking with clicks. What could he possibly be saying? When shimmering hummingbirds take a drink from our morning glories, they leave me completely undone. Wildlife and wonder provoke me to worship. Recently I was at the Aquarium of the Pacific, and I saw sea dragons for the first time in my life. Wonder literally knocked me to my knees. What kind of God invents sea dragons? David said, "The works of the Lord are great. Studied by all those who have pleasure in them." [12]

See What Everyone Else Misses

There are many worthwhile things to watch everywhere you look. Maybe you live in a crowded city and there is not much nature about you. If that's the case you can watch God's best work—people. I like to pray for people, imagining their stories, wondering how God is going to merge their stories into the story of Jesus. If you love to watch television there are biographies, nature shows, science programs, and documentaries of all types. Do we dash through our days feeding on whatever noise is available, allowing music, television, talk shows, newspapers, tabloids, and movie producers to dictate our thought life? Are we continually barraged and emotionally assaulted by noise? Or do we carefully choose our own mental diet? Have we learned to nourish our soul on silence?

Norman Vincent Peale, when he was pastoring the Marble Collegiate Church, always scheduled one minute of silence in his worship services. People who attended often said that one minute of silence was the most significant portion of the service. God invites us to "Be still, and know that I am God."[13] If stillness helps us know God, we should learn to seek it, to enjoy it. Noise and busyness keep us from revelation. They are the enemy's weapon of choice against each of us.

Beware the barrenness of busyness. The object of silence is not negation of self, like oriental philosophy teaches, but *revelation* of the heart and mind of Jesus. I pray weekly with some friends who always take fifteen to twenty minutes of silence together to meditate on the Word of God before we pray. When you're not used to silence it can be very intimidating. The biggest challenge is to clear our minds of our to-do lists, our personal prayer lists—our mental freeway is bottlenecked, and it takes a while to learn to get really still before God.

Thomas Kelly says,

Many of the things we are doing seem so important to us. We haven't been able to say no to them because they seem so important. But if we centered down, as the phrase goes, and live in that Holy Silence which is deeper than life, and take our life program into the silent places of the heart with complete openness, ready to do, ready to renounce, according to His leading. Then many of the things we are doing lose their vitality for us.[14]

Many things have lost their vitality for me in the light of God's presence. I used to be fiercely competitive. (You would never want to play the game of Risk against me. I was always the missionary taking over the world.) Positions I once held and thought important have faded like spent flowers. Things that once consumed my time and energy now do not even appear on my radar screen.

Author Ken Gire suggests three habits of the heart that will nurture a reflective life. He suggests reading the moment, reflecting on the moment (seeing below the surface), and responding to the moment (giving it a place in your heart, allowing it to grow upward to God and outward to others).[15] Jesus was a master of reading the moment. Little things did not escape His attention. He was not so preoccupied being the Son of God that He did not notice the little lady with the issue of blood touching him in the midst of an enormous crowd. His thought life was not so crowded that He could not read the moment when little children were coming up to Him to be blessed. Jesus never allowed a crowded thought life to obscure the moment.

For almost a decade now, I have watched my pastor around little children. Despite a huge congregation, Pastor John Huffman never sidesteps the children. He reads the moment well. It might just be a nanosecond touch on the forehead or a high five, but he remembers their names, looks them straight in the eyes, and always makes them feel valuable.

It is important not to simply read the moment but to reflect on it and then respond. This is as true in our reading of Scripture as in our daily living. Recently a friend and I were approached at the beach by a homeless woman begging for a meal. My friend said she would be happy to buy the woman a meal. As we walked to the restaurant, we took time to reflect on her life. We asked her about her story, what her days were like, what were the hardest parts of being a homeless woman. How did people respond to her? How did the police treat her? Linda talked freely. Afterward we prayed with her a very simple prayer about the Lord protecting her from harm. Linda was Jesus in one of "His many distressing disguises," as Mother Teresa used to say. We gave her lunch, but she gave us the gift of realizing how small our challenges really were in light of her daily life.

That night in my warm, cozy bed, next to a tender-hearted, faithful husband, I reflected on my life compared to hers. I responded to the Lord with gratitude and humility. There was really no difference between that homeless woman and myself. I was not better, smarter, more whole. Both of us desperately need Jesus every moment of our lives. Both of us are desperate and hopeless without Him.

KEEPING FOCUSED ON JESUS

God has given us various resources to help focus our thought life on Jesus. Previous generations would have coveted the smorgasbord of options available to us. I listen to worship tapes as I drive to keep my mind stayed on Jesus. No matter what style of music you enjoy, from the Brooklyn Tabernacle Choir to gentle acoustic music, there is a worship series for every palate. Keep your soul steeped in what is good. Keep your idle moments out of neutral. If you are stopped at a crosswalk, pray a blessing on those who are crossing. If you have to wait in line at the post office, silently talk to God about the people in front of you. Everything you look at can become a silent prompt to pray. You can talk to Jesus all day long without ever speaking a word out loud.

The story is told that a group of theologians met to discuss the verse, "Pray without ceasing." As theologians are tempted to do, they waxed eloquent about what that verse could possibly mean. They all conceded it was impossible to pray without ceasing. A young maid came in to serve them and overheard. "Why, that's the simplest verse in the world," the maid declared. The men were amazed. "How could you possibly pray without ceasing?" they asked. "Why, the busier I am the more I pray. If I have to sweep, I ask the Lord to sweep away the clutter in my life. If I am doing the dishes, I ask the Lord to wash me clean. When I iron, I thank God that He is going to present me to Jesus without spot or wrinkle. The more I have to do, the more I pray."

Listening to the Word on tape as you drive is another way to let your mind marinate on Jesus and His Word. Dramatic versions of the New Testament on tape are great for the car. I find it amazing how much better I respond to listening to the Word than to simply reading it. If you drive a lot, listen to classic books about God on tape. Or record a book of the Bible or a classic for your grandchildren who may live far away. Keep your mind and heart fixed on Jesus by being occupied with Him.

Cultivate a listening heart. A young teenager recently

accepted a dare not to talk for a whole year. He realized how little he really listened. He, like most of us, was usually busy formulating an answer while other people talked. Listening is an art few of us learn. In our house we intentionally create silent zones when we watch TV. We mute all commercials. You would not believe the beauty of silence every five or ten minutes. Reflecting on what we have watched allows us to truly see. Silence is restorative. We can hear with greater ease when our minds and hearts are not continually bombarded by noise.

Jesus invites us to fill our minds with Him. We will be transformed into His likeness as we spend our thought life on Him. Surround yourself with people who have no greater joy than to talk about Him. Author Frederick Buechner says, "the trouble oftentimes with religious people is that they try to be more spiritual than God Himself."[16] I do not mean religious people who pepper every other phrase with "Praise the Lord." I mean people who authentically know that Jesus is the treasure, the Bible is the treasure map, we are all clues, and life is the hunt. The kind of people that Malachi talks about when he says,

> Then those who feared the Lord spoke to one another, and the Lord listened and heard them; so a book of remembrance was written before Him for those who fear the Lord and who meditate on His name. "They shall be Mine," says the Lord of hosts, "on the day that I make them My jewels. And I will spare them as a man spares his own son who serves him."[17]

Five

Jesus, the Heart of Our Salvation

———

*There was never any other way to escape death
than for men to flee to Christ.*[1]

—JOHN CALVIN

You will be tempted to think this story is straight out of *Ripley's Believe or Not!*, but it happened not that long ago, right off our coast. A Navy photographer was on a boat sharing Jesus with a friend. The friend said, "I am glad that's working for you, but I just do not sense a real need for God in my life." No sooner had he gotten the words out of his mouth then a wave rose over the boat and swept both men out to sea. Another wave came just as suddenly and swept them back onto the boat. They lay on the deck breathlessly looking at each other. "What was that you were saying about Jesus?" the man asked. Not long after that experience, he committed his life to Christ and married his live-in girlfriend.

I tell the next unbelievable story hesitantly, prefaced by a severe warning. Playing with a Ouija board is the kind of practice strictly forbidden by God. Avoid it like the plague, treat it like nuclear fallout. In other words do not ever go anywhere near it. I tell this story only to show the length God will go to in order to get people to Jesus. A friend of mine was desperate for truth and clueless (that will become obvious) where to look for it. She had tried many new age spiritualities and found them all empty. Incredibly, she ended up investigating the claims of Jesus because an Ouija board, of all things. She asked, "What is truth?" The board amazingly answered back, "Jesus."

The Father can bring anyone to Jesus and use absolutely any means. I have heard of people turning to Christ through musicals I had thought blasphemous. One famous actor came to Jesus because he used to sit up late at night due to insomnia, making fun of the antics and appearance of a certain Christian television personality. While he was mocking, the Holy Spirit was busy convicting and drawing him. One person in England met Christ while reading a sermon printed on some newspaper wrapping that bundled up his fish and chips. I have even heard of someone convicted by the Holy Spirit through a car commercial. When God sets out to do a thing, He does not have to have all your theological ducks in a row. The message or the messenger can be faulty, but God is determined to accomplish His pleasure. And that pleasure is for the world to know His Son.

That pleasure and passion of God burns within us as well. My family and I live on a mountain with a cityscape sprawling around us for miles. Sometimes at night I will go out on the deck to pray over the city, longing for Jesus to be known and loved in Ventura County. Occasionally Joel

will join me in extending our hands out over the city, blessing all the children who perhaps were not blessed by their
parents as they were tucked into bed. I can think of nothing sweeter than people coming to know and love Christ.
The yearning for cities and nations to know Him occupies
much of my prayer life and thinking.

If we love Jesus, we will applaud absolutely anything that
leads people to a genuine encounter with Him. Our hearts
will be so passionate about people finding Jesus that we
never raise an eyebrow at someone else's approach.
Someone once criticized how Dwight L. Moody brought
people to Jesus. Moody replied, "I do not like it either, but I
like it better than how you are not bringing people to Jesus."
People who are critical are rarely good fishers of men. You
can criticize or you can fish, but you cannot do both.

One pastor friend has started churches in several local
bars. Other pastors were mortified. Given Jesus' history, I
think He would be quite at home ministering in a bar. "It's
not the well that need a physician but the sick" (see Matt.
9:12), Jesus would again remind us. There are many luminous and creative ways to proclaim Jesus. I am always
impressed with the enormous creativity of Campus Crusade
for Christ and Youth With A Mission. They have been particularly successful in drawing outside the lines, thinking
outside the four walls of church with activities such as aqua-
farming, character-building curricula for public schools, and
business development seminars in second- and third-world
countries. The possibilities to creatively proclaim Christ are
limitless. A famous and delicious hamburger chain here in

California even prints scripture references on the bottom of their cups.

Having said all that, we would be less than honest if we did not admit we have not been particularly successful in the Western world actually getting people to Jesus. The statistics are shocking and heartbreaking. How can it be that according to some statistics, the net conversion rate in America for the last ten years is zero? According to futurologist Leonard Sweet, there is not one county in the United States that has a higher percentage of churched people than it did a decade ago.[2] Statistics indicate that most church growth even in the megachurches is transfer growth, not new convert growth.

Have we missed something? Are our own hearts so lukewarm toward the desirability of Christ that Jesus really is no big deal to us, just one of many halfhearted loyalties? The desire of nations, Jesus, the Lamb slain from the foundation of the world, richly deserves the reward of His sacrifice. Jesus is worthy of being adored and obeyed by all. Do we live for the satisfaction of His heart? Does our heart yearn to see Jesus become the talk of our city, the talk of the bedroom and boardroom, the talk of our playgrounds and prisons? Do we crave to see our neighborhoods filled with new disciples eagerly sitting at Jesus' feet?

SOMETHING IS DEFINITELY MISSING

Our current methods would benefit from a fresh assessment. It is ludicrous to keep doing the same thing and expect a different result. One of the more familiar ways we attempt to draw people to Christ is at church, at the close of a service. While music plays softly, everyone is asked to bow their heads and close their eyes. Those desiring to accept the gift of salvation are asked to either raise their hands or to look up at the pastor. In some churches people are invited to the front to say the sinner's prayer. Thousands of people have genuinely come to Jesus in this manner, so I do not want to make light of anyone's entrance into the life of Christ.

But according to pollster George Barna, a large majority of those who presently "make decisions" cannot be found in church eight weeks from the date of their decision.[3] To be fair, we must admit Jesus had His own recidivism problem. When His followers found out the cost, many forsook Him. But those who are leaving us are not leaving because the cost is too high, but because the cost is too low. We are rarely presenting a Savior worth dying for.

WOULD JESUS RECOGNIZE OUR MESSAGE OR METHODS?

Would Jesus recognize our methods or our message? Have we made assumptions that are not biblical? What cultural factors do we accommodate that lessen commitment? It is easier to unquestioningly parrot the standard appeals rather than hold them up to the light of Scripture. If we take even a casual glance at the evangelistic methodology of Jesus, we see something very different from most of our methods. And we often find an entirely different message as well.

JESUS WAS NEVER IN A HURRY

One of the striking things we notice in the gospel narratives is that Jesus was never in a hurry. He was never frantic, never desperate. He never forced someone into following Him. If anything, He seemed to make it all rather difficult. In our haste we perform spiritual caesarian sections instead of allowing natural birth. We often usurp the convicting power of the Holy Spirit and offer people a hurried entrance into the kingdom. "Here, just say this prayer. Now, you're saved." I wonder have they actually encountered Jesus? In our press to save the world, to collect impressive statistics that validate our ministries, do we rush people into making commitments too quickly? Do they really know who they are committing themselves to? Do we?

In contrast to Paul, who had a dynamic encounter with God on the Damascus Road, the disciples were slow of heart to believe. Yet we often take the experience of Paul as normative conversion and forget that the disciples, dull of heart like us, came to believing faith over a period of time by being exposed to Jesus. Best-selling author Kathleen Norris was once asked how she could stand going to church, how she could stand the hypocrisy of Christians. She replied, "The only hypocrite I have to worry about on Sunday morning is myself." She goes on to say:

The congregation in Lemmon, South Dakota, has seen me come and go, mercifully they've allowed my conversion to unfold in their midst without pestering me to see if I have been saved in just the right way . . . this is why the teachings of St. Augustine are so precious to me. He helps me see, in the lengthy story of his own conversion—with its fits and starts, its meanderings and deep desire for faith—that mine has been a traditional Christian journey.[4]

We, like the congregation in South Dakota, need to be patient with the Holy Spirit's work in someone's life. We must keep declaring the beauty and excellence of Jesus and leave the results to God. We are not responsible for the results of our obedience. *We are not salvation detectives.* Salvation belongs to the Lord. We simply are called to love and proclaim His Lordship.

Once after a meeting in an Arab country, a friend wrote back to America and said, "I'll tell you in five years who came to the Lord tonight." I loved it. No inflated figures, no hype, no empire-building stories about our great anointing and effectiveness—just gutsy, honest assessment. What if we put a moratorium on salvation statistics and spent the time instead simply talking about the wonder of Jesus?

I once watched uncomfortably as someone railroaded an Iranian friend of mine into saying the sinner's prayer. She wasn't praying on her own initiative, she was pressured into doing it because she was asked a trick question: "Is there any reason you wouldn't want to accept God's offer of salvation right now?" How much sweeter it would have been to love her until she asked why and let the Holy Spirit stir desire in her heart. Are we more like telemarketers closing the deal or allies with the Holy Spirit, the ultimate heart opener?

Dr. Joe Aldrich, former president of Multnomah, once asked the Lord to put a searching nonbeliever in his life. The very next day a high school friend whom Joe had not seen in thirty years walked into his office. Bob had no idea how he got there; he just felt compelled to pull in the driveway. He asked the secretary what the school was about, and she mentioned that Joe Aldrich was the president. Bob recognized the name from high school and walked into Joe's office and proceeded to pour out his heart. His life was falling apart at the seams. Joe recognized that this man was his answer to prayer. What happened next, Joe tells best in his own words:

> I backed up the evangelical dump truck and pulled the lever. I kept the heat on until he prayed the prayer. I gave him a beautiful new Bible, some quick words of assurance, and sent him on his way. I never heard from him again. He was not ready and I was not sensitive. I made his pilgrimage to the cross more difficult for the next person who tries to point him in that direction.[5]

We once ran an ad for a roommate. A young man named Dwayne applied for the room, and we liked him right off the bat. He ended up finding another home. Then a few weeks later, there was a knock on our door. It was Dwayne. "You people really seem to know God, and I was wondering if . . ." For four months we met with Dwayne to answer his questions as he read through the New Testament. He put little sticky-notes on Scriptures he did not understand. Each time we asked him if he was ready to pray. "No, not yet." One afternoon I got a call. "I just want you to know, I got down on my knees and accepted Christ." I was thrilled. This was no hasty decision made in a moment of emotional stirring. Dwayne carefully considered the claims of Christ before he committed. He counted the cost.

Is Our Message Jesus?

Perhaps the reason so many decisions for Christ do not last is because our message is not about Jesus; it is primarily about man. Our accent is on the wrong syllable; our emphasis is in the wrong place. We often ask, "Where will you spend eternity?" Instead of asking *with Whom*? We are often more motivated to save man from the ramifications of sin than to satisfy the heart of God.

When Jesus is the subject of the sentence, the whole story shifts. We recognize His authority, His supremacy, His absolute right to lay claim to our lives, His worth of our unswerving loyalty and obedience. When man is the subject of our appeal, Jesus becomes merely a means to an end. He becomes the solution to our needs, our desires. Jesus becomes the ultimate therapy for our diseased souls. We end up always getting better but never getting well.

A man-centered gospel carries tremendous risks. We

can harden hearts and inoculate people against the true convicting presence of the Holy Spirit. When Jesus is not the focus, people end up thinking they've met God when all they've been exposed to is religious rhetoric.

Jimmy Carter, during his presidential campaign, said he was born-again. The press, not sure what he meant, called University of Chicago church historian Martin Marty, asking for a definition. Marty thought for a moment and said, "Well, the whole South is born-again." Could a whole region truly be born-again? Or do we mean that just about everybody there has at one time or another said the sinner's prayer? Is that all we are really aiming for? "Repeat after me" conversions do not seem to merit the drastic price of Calvary. Dallas Willard describes the fallacy of this kind of thinking: "We may not have done or become anything positive to speak of. But when we come to heaven's gate, they will not be able to find a reason to keep us out. The mere record of a magical moment of mental assent will open the door."[6] Did Jesus go to the cross for us to simply give a mere magical moment of mental assent?

My pastor has a friend who prayed once to receive Christ and then went on with life as usual. When asked a week later why he was not attending church, he said, "Oh, I already took care of all that last week. Why should I return?" While his response is humorous, I do not think it should come as some great surprise. We have deafened scores of people to the claims of Christ with an easy, minimalist presentation. We tell people about the Lordship of

Jesus incrementally. By the time we get to finally mentioning His Lordship and discipleship, our converts are bored and onto other things.

Recently I changed my long-distance provider. Before I finished my telephone conversation I was sent to a third-party verifier. They wanted to be sure I knew exactly what it was I was signing up for. Did I understand what they offered? Did I really want their service? We might do well to follow their example. Converts need to know *Who* exactly it is they are agreeing to accept. It is an error to present salvation as simply a gift to be received or a prayer to pray, instead of as a Person who enters us and takes full charge of the house.

JESUS' EMBARRASSING APPROACH

If Jesus had been on the campaign trail soliciting votes, He would have given his campaign advisers a serious case of hives. Jesus said all the wrong things to attract a crowd: "If any one desires to come after Me, let him deny himself, and take up his cross, and follow Me."[7] How many hands would go up to accept Christ if that were the invitation? Or how about, "Sell all that you have and distribute to the poor, and you will have treasure in heaven; and come, follow Me."[8] Or the worst: "Unless you eat the flesh of the Son of Man and drink His blood, you have no life in you."[9] Our conversion statistics might be fewer if Jesus or Paul gave the altar call. They might be fewer, but they might last.

Jesus rarely had a standard response. Each reply was tailored to the individual. Jesus said to the demon-possessed man He'd just delivered, "Go home to your friends, and tell them what great things the Lord has done for you, and how He has had compassion on you."[10] Others He told *not* to tell.[11] He made salvation seem absolutely impossible to the rich young ruler. He made it easy for the woman taken in adultery. "Go and sin no more."[12] I wonder, if we were sensitive to Jesus' heart for the individual, how much more varied we'd be in how we present the gospel. Jesus demonstrated the fact that there is no "one size fits all" when it comes to becoming His friend. Our particular method of response is not as important as our understanding and heart engagement about who Jesus actually is.

SALVATION IS A PERSON

Salvation is not mere agreement with a theological construct. You do not convert by just agreeing intellectually with the "Four Spiritual Laws," by opening your eyes, or raising your hand, and then going about your life as you always have. Salvation is a Person. Jesus said to the woman at the well, "If you knew the gift of God, and who it is who says to you, 'Give Me a drink,' you would have asked Him, and He would have given you living water."[13] Hudson Taylor comments on the passage: "'If any man thirst let Him come to Me and drink.' Who does not thirst? Who has not mind thirsts, heart thirsts, soul thirsts, or body thirsts? . . . 'Come unto me and remain thirsty?' Ah no! 'Come to me and drink.' What, can Jesus meet my need? Yes and more than meet it . . . Jesus can meet all, all and more than meet."[14] Jesus was not offering the woman at the well a gift separate *from* Himself, merely a new way of thinking and responding to life. He was offering her the gift *of* Himself, the Prince of Life. He did not try to refine the woman's theology or give her a more accurate view of the finer nuances of Messiahship. He offered her Himself. "Ask *Me* for living Water . . . Whoever drinks of *Me*, will never thirst again." To present salvation as a transaction or an agreement of intellectual assent, rather than an encounter with the Living Christ, is meaningless. Jesus does not give us a ticket to get into heaven. He gives us entrance to Himself. As British author P. T. Forsyth observes: "To be a Christian is not to attach one's salvation to a grand individual . . . it is to enter Christ."[15]

Hudson Taylor writes his sister of the joy of discovering this truth:

Abiding, not striving nor struggling; looking off to Him; trusting Him for present power; resting in the love of an almighty Savior, in the joy of a complete salvation . . . I seem to have got to the edge only, but of a boundless sea; to have sipped only, but of that which fully satisfies. Christ literally all seems to me, now the power, the only power for service, the only ground for unchanging joy . . . it is not a striving to have faith . . . but a looking off to the Faithful One seems all we need; a resting in the Loved One entirely, for time and eternity.[16]

Salvation is a Person. Jesus declared with clear-faced certainty, "I am the way, the truth, and the life. No one comes to the Father except through Me."[17] Salvation is not a way of being, a path of enlightened spirituality. It is not a path, but a Person. Jesus *is* the way, He does not have a way. He does not merely give us a map out of the labyrinthine maze of our confusion. He is the way. E. Stanley Jones found himself in a jungle where there was no path. His guide furiously hacked away through the dense underbrush, trying to clear a way. Jones said to his guide, "Are you sure this leads to the path?" The guide answered, "Bhanna, right now, *I am* your path." Jesus is our path, our way.

Recently I went with a friend to a corn maze. I had been there ten minutes and was more than ready to leave. I loathe puzzles. If you are going to use brainpower, solve something that *matters*. The sun was pelting malignant rays on our hatless heads, the ocean breeze was dead in the water, and we had forgotten sunscreen. I kept thinking to myself, *We paid to do this?* We went around and around like little hamsters in a cage. I was a grumpy and miserable hamster, feeling entirely unsanctified. We only had a few little pieces of a map. Clues were strewn about the two-acre plot in little mailboxes. Mercifully, we finally found a person who was a guide. He knew every inch of that maze. He became our map, and he led us straight to the exit. I was so happy to find him, I could have fallen at his feet.

Jesus does not hand us a set of directions. He does not hide the clues and hope we find them at some point in our journey. He gives us Himself. He is the way, and there is no other. He is not one of many ways, He is *the* way. There is salvation in no other. Jesus claims total exclusivity in being the Savior of the world.

JESUS IS TRUTH

Jesus is the truth. We see that truth best in Jesus as He hangs on the cross for us. In Him we see the dire truth about sin, about ourselves, about Him. We see the serious price of sin. We realize that our rebellion cost God the life of His most priceless Son. We see that the law came from Moses, but mercy and truth kissed themselves in Christ. We see that truth is not a set of principles to embrace; it is not a doctrinal position to affirm. Truth is not ortho-doxy defined by an ecclesiastical authority. Truth is a Person, and that Person is Jesus. Leonard Sweet puts it like this:

> Truth is not a principle or a proposition, but a Person. Truth is not rules and regulations but a relationship. God did not send us a statement but a Savior. God did not send us a principle but a presence. Surrendering to Jesus is not a subscription to some "article of faith," but merging one's personal story into the story of the Son of God and Savior of the World.[18]

All we are asked to do is be willing to be completely dependent on Him, looking to Him in faith for our every need. We might not have the right feelings, the right atti-tude, the right actions, the right anything. But we trust Him to be for us all that God requires of us.

JESUS IS THE LIFE

Jesus is life. He does not have a life, He is life itself. He illustrates how His life is lived in us, by using the metaphor of a vine and branches. Jesus, in John 15, calls Himself the true vine and calls us the branches. We are merged into and grafted onto Him, wholly dependent on Him for life and fruit. Hudson Taylor many years ago talked about this relatedness:

> How great seemed my mistake in having wished to get the sap, the fullness out of Him. I saw not only that Jesus would never leave me, but I was a member of His body, of His flesh and of His bones. The vine now I see, is not the root merely, but all . . . root, stem, branches, twigs, leaves, flowers, fruit: and Jesus is not only that: He is soil and sunshine, air and showers and ten thousand times more than we have ever dreamed, wished for or needed.[19]

Salvation is all Jesus. We cannot by our own effort add a thing to it. He has given Himself completely for us and to us.

Just in case there was any confusion, any thinking that we could live by our own wits, our own striving to please God, our own internal discipline in keeping God's laws, Jesus says flatly, "Without Me you can do nothing."[20] Author Harry Blamires says, "In the Christ life, nothing, nothing at all, can be purchased at the do-it-yourself shop."[21] Jesus becomes for us everything required by God for our salvation. He is the all-sufficient One, our righteousness, our fruitfulness, our completeness. The

Hebrew word for salvation means to make wide, to make sufficient. Jesus is so spacious that Eugene Peterson says, "All of God fits within Him without crowding."[22] We fit as well in Him, with all our brokenness, our frail egos, our thumb-sucking immaturity and coddled fears. We are in Him who is spacious with wholeness, health, and vitality.

All we are asked to do is abide in His love and accept His commandments. And what are Jesus' commandments? To love the Lord our God with all our heart and all our soul, and to love our neighbor as ourselves. Two things we could never do apart from Him living His life in us. You see, Jesus is not only the way, the truth, the life; He is also love itself (John 14:6). There is no command ever given us that Jesus is not the one who performs in us what we could never do by ourselves.

Salvation is intentionally quite impossible apart from Jesus. God has designed our moment-by-moment life to be impossible to live right without Jesus. Our everyday is just as important as our eternity. So Jesus is for us, right now, this very moment. There is no activity of your life outside the scope of His love and interest. There is no moment that He will not save you.

Appealing to Man's Interests or God's Interests?

If Jesus is the center and circumference, the entirety of our salvation, how did we reduce Him to a tidy little salvation packet and a canned "repeat after me" prayer? Pastor Paris

Reidhead lays the blame squarely in the lap of evangelicalism. Reidhead sobs and thunders against evangelicals' descent into humanism, the miasma he calls "the betrayal of the ages."[23] Through the progressive influence of philosophical thought, Christianity over the last two hundred years has become increasingly man-centered. Strong undertows of philosophy have eroded our once clearly Christ-centered message.

We are more affected by philosophy in our presentation of Christ than we realize. The world is much more powerfully affected by some obscure philosopher hidden away writing books a hundred years ago than by presidents, kings, or Hollywood. Nietzsche said, "Power is all," and Hitler was the result. Existentialism said, "Sensuality is all. Man is a glandular animal whose ecstasy is all," and Hollywood was the result. Science said, "Knowledge is all," and despair was the result. Scripture says that the end of all things is the glory of God.

As humanist ideals swept the globe, liberals of the 1850s felt that great thoughts and noble aspirations were all Christianity had left to offer. They felt all they could do was put a little sugar in the bitter coffee of life. They could not change the fact that the road of life went nowhere; they could only put some shock absorbers on your car as you went. Fundamentalists, on the other hand, embraced a vivid belief in the deity of Christ, the inspiration of the Bible, the literalness of heaven and hell. But by the second generation, fundamentalists, affected by humanism, merely asked for an intellectual assent to a formula of doctrine. We were asked to agree with doctrinal truths instead of believing in Jesus, the truth. The emphasis became believing the right things instead of entering the life of the right One.

Humanism has slowly seeped into mainstream evangelicalism for the past two centuries. It eventually engulfed evangelicals to the point where we now say, "Accept Jesus so you can go to heaven." We have been unconsciously affected by philosophy that puts man at the center of all things. It's no longer all about You, Jesus, it's all about you, neighbor. Come to Jesus, and He will make your life more successful. He'll help your marriage. He'll straighten out your kids and help you sleep at night. Jesus is now the ultimate therapist, and we encourage people to climb up on His couch to make their lives secure. It is, according to Reidhead, the ultimate appeal to selfishness. Are we biblical in our call for repentance? Do we want people to come to Christ "to the praise of His glorious grace" or because we want to spare them hell and secure for them an eternally nice day?

God is creating a Church that will be focused on the greatness and excellence of Jesus. We will be asking how we fit into His holy ambitions, rather than how He fits into our never-ending needs and desires. We will, with Paul, proclaim Him. We will want Him. We will be willing to die for Him. We will not count our lives precious but will freely and with abandon declare His splendor, His excellence, and His supremacy. Our message will be relentlessly on target, Jesus and Jesus alone. Jesus is our future and our wholeness. Our destiny is comprehensively linked to His.

BRINGING PEOPLE TO JESUS

Jesus is all we really have to offer. Author Chip Brogden says:

> When we hear the phrase, "bring people to Christ," we are apt to think in terms of tent revivals, evangelistic meetings, and missionary campaigns . . . The whole aim and purpose of God is to bring us to Christ—not once, but continually, daily, hour by hour, minute by minute. Just as a wildly spinning compass eventually points to true north, so the Holy Spirit is arranging our lives and ordering our steps so that we are constantly being brought back to our "true north," centered and focused on and into *Christ*, forever being made to see our sufficiency is of Him, that He is the Author and the Finisher of our faith, that we are complete in Him, and seated with Him in the heavenly places. As believers, we ought always to encourage and exhort one another, bringing the saint and the sinner alike *back to Christ* (either for the first time or for the one thousandth time), back to their Source, back to their Life . . . The goal of all Spirit-led ministry is to bring people *to Christ*, tenaciously, even relentlessly, making the most of every opportunity to give them the Testimony of Jesus Christ.[24]

We have no higher calling than to bring people to Jesus. He is not a means to an end, even if that end is good. He is both the beginning and the end, the Alpha, the Omega, and all the letters in between. Jesus is not a product we market to consumers. He is Lord of history, Lord of time, Lord of all. You will not find Him on a shelf with cold remedies.

When people come to Jesus, yes, He will save them, heal them, and bring them joy. But He does not exist for us. We exist for Him. Christ is not a means to our end. As British theologian P. T. Forsythe says, "Jesus is not only faith's object but also faith's world. He becomes our universe that feels and knows and makes us what we are."[25]

Six

Jesus, the Heart of Our Relationships

All relationships are mediated through Him.
I never think simply of what I am going to do with
you, to you, and for you . . . but of what will be done
by you and Jesus with me, to me and for me. The
ground and strength and promise of all our fellowship
is in Jesus Christ alone.[1]

—DIETRICH BONHOEFFER

I happened to call one evening after dinner. As I listened to him pick up the phone, my heart stopped cold. He said, "I think this is it. I am dying." I swallowed hard, turning decisively. "I am calling the ambulance immediately. We are getting in the car right now, and we'll be there in twenty minutes." We sped to his city, my mind racing with what might meet us when we arrived. We got to his house right after the ambulance. My dad was bleeding to death. He was rushed to a nearby hospital. There was no time to take him to a better hospital back in my own city. Life was pouring out of him, and every second counted.

Blood was gushing out of him—so much blood that the nursing staff left bedpans full of it on the floor. My queasy stomach threatened to stage a revolt. The doctors asked me to tell my dad he had two options. He would either die in the next ten minutes or he could have surgery and would probably die during the operation.

My dad was understandably petrified. The prospect of an anesthetic for his agony was the determining factor. After the useless operation, he hovered in and out of a coma for two weeks, terrified to die, too sick to live.

He had tubes sticking out of every possible place in his body. I had repeatedly told the intensive care team that he wanted no "heroic" measures. Doctors gave me patronizing looks as they inserted yet one more piece of equipment. "Everything we are doing is within standard parameters," they said. My dad's excellent insurance perhaps fueled their expensive decisions. Before he died, the doctors used every piece of equipment intensive care had available.

Every day I dragged myself to the hospital alone, feeling crushed with the weight of a million "if only's." My parents had divorced when I was a baby. I had never lived with my dad. We had just resumed a relationship about seven years before. I had not loved my dad well. I was just learning what age teaches: that my dad had loved me as he had been able. Now he was dying, and he still resisted talking about God. I staggered through the days of his dying, never quite finding my legs or my tongue.

One day a close friend gently asked me a puzzling

question: *"So who is going with you to the hospital?"* Who was going with me? Who would *want* to go with me? The thought had not even *remotely* occurred to me. My days were painful enough without dragging someone else into the picture. I was a "Marlboro Man," braving the harsh elements by myself. I grew up singing, "Though none go with me, still I will follow." Companionship in the face of tragedy was a foreign idea.

I had forgotten that Jesus sent out the disciples two by two. If you pressed me, I privately thought this two-by-two business was a terrible waste of efficiency. Having grown up mostly in small churches, I thought God only attracted a tiny remnant. If we paired everybody up, we would lessen our potential by 50 percent. But Ecclesiastes says, "Two are better than one, because they have a good reward for their labor. For if they fall, one will lift up his companion."[2] God made us for relationship. He crafted our hearts to need others, especially during a time of tragedy. I was clueless to this powerful dynamic of companionship.

My friend refused my no, and went with me the next day and several times later. She knew exactly what to do. She was a fish in water, moving naturally and with ease. She comforted my dad as he resisted death. I was amazed that just someone's presence could provide such rock-solid strength. When I could barely face my father's future on my own, God in His tenderness sent a skillful prayer companion to be with me.

RELATIONSHIP—THE HEART
OF THE UNIVERSE

More than we long for food, money, or success, we long to not be alone. Relationship is at the heart of the universe. Phillip Yancey once said that when it is all said and done, all we ever really wanted was to be loved and desired by the Maker of all things. If you question that relationship is the deepest craving of the human heart, just listen to any country-and-western music station for five minutes. People fear loneliness so much that they stay in abusive relationships; they marry people they do not love; they join gangs; they violate their own sexual purity; they do *anything* to not be alone. We crave companionship at all costs.

Of course, God had a whole lot more in mind for us than to just be warm bodies to each other. The relationship for which we were made, the relationship our heart never ceases to crave, is very specific. We are barely into the first chapter of the story when we encounter a significant fact: "Let *Us* make man in Our image."[3] Making man was a relational affair from the very beginning. We were born in the womb of the greatest relationship the galaxies have ever known. God the Father, God the Son, and God the Holy Spirit created man *out of* their relationship, *for* their relationship. The theme is consistent all through Scripture: God made us for Himself.

Revelation tells us we were made for His pleasure.[4] Colossians says that all things were made by Him and for

Him.⁵ We were not simply made to be relational but to have relationship with a specific Person. Every relationship that excludes that specific Person falls short of its intended destiny.

George MacDonald makes the bold observation that relationship is at the heart of the universe:

> The bond of the universe . . . is the devotion of the Son to the Father. It is the life of the universe. It is not the fact that God created all things, that makes the universe whole; but that He through who He created them, loves Him perfectly, is eternally content in His father, is satisfied to be, because His Father is with Him . . . for the very beginnings of unity there must be two, without Christ therefore, there could be no universe.⁶

Jesus is *completely* devoted to His Father. There is not the slightest shred of disloyalty in Him. He is no Absalom,⁷ seeking to woo and win the hearts of Israel, and usurp and conquer his Father's throne. His glory and joy is in seeing the Father glorified. In John 17, Jesus prays, "Glorify your Son, that Your Son also may glorify You."⁸

All that you can see, feel, and touch, and worlds beyond our knowing, were born out of an indivisible unity of the Father, Son, and Holy Spirit. "Let us make man in our image,"⁹ God said. The image we bear is not composed of facial or external features. It can rarely be said that we have our Father's eyes. It is not as if we walk, run, or hold our head similar to the way God does. Oh no! It is that our inner being is made like Him. We were made a trinity, body, soul, and spirit. We were made for indivisible relationship with Him and with each other. We were made to be a part of Him and of each other. In Jesus' prayer in John 17 we see the marvelous intertwining of the Trinity. Into that ultimate unity a universe is born. Into that ultimate unity we were embraced through the cross to become heirs of God and joint heirs with Christ. Out of our oneness with Christ, we have the capacity to be friends with one another. Jesus organizes His kingdom with gifts of friendship. Where Jesus is, friendships form. Where Jesus is, friendships last.

I have been privileged to direct and write several plays and productions in my life. Directing gives me great pleasure. I love the creativity and energy involved in bringing out the best in a cast. I enjoy taking a cast of strangers and giving them a common vision and a place to express their gifts. I particularly love watching friendships form as people discover the joy of working together. Sadly though, when the production is finished, the closeness of a cast often dissipates. I have watched this dynamic repeat itself again and again, and scratched my head in puzzlement. I have come to the conclusion that when we are gathered around a project, not a Person, our relationships rarely endure. When Jesus is the heart of our relationships, our friendships endure, because *He* endures. We can never exhaust Him, never run out of things to delight about in Him.

When Jesus Is the Heart of Our Friendships, They Stay Fresh

Have you ever been in a restaurant and watched two people eat silently with each other? They may speak two sentences in an hour. They budget their words, like a miser counting money. Then one of them will stand up and say, "It was great to see you. Let's do this again sometime." Was their meal emotionally satisfying? Could life really be that vacuous? When we cramp our souls into tight boxes, of course we have nothing to discuss.

But when Jesus is the heart of our friendships, we never run out of things that delight. I have several close friends around the world. We have known each other for many years, and our friendships stay fresh and sweet. They stay that way because Jesus is the heart of our joy in each other. What we like best about each other is Jesus. We have no greater joy than to talk about Him, to compare notes, and make observations. We are companions in the sacred order of the burning heart. We are passionate about Jesus, and our friendships endure because He endures. I count these friendships among my great treasures in life. I rarely walk away from a conversation with these friends without knowing Jesus better and understanding life more fully.

He Helps Us Not to Use People

I have a Hindu friend whom I deeply love. I am *not* her friend in order to introduce her to Jesus, although that is my highest longing for her. I am her friend because Jesus has allowed me to know His heart for her. If she never becomes a lover of Jesus, my love for her will not waver. Our friendship is not based on an eventual outcome, but on Jesus' very full heart of love toward her.

I fear that often we are only nice to people in order to convert them. When they do not show any signs of responding, we move on to someone else more receptive. We often are Machiavellian in our friendships with pre-Christians. We must ask ourselves, "Is my heart toward a neighbor only soft because I perceive they might become a Christian?" Our tenderness toward people must be because God's unfailing love is toward them. We are not responsible for their response to God. We are responsible simply to love. How might Jesus be welcomed if we determined to endlessly love the world without regard for response! Someone once said, "Love them until they ask you why." That is the best counsel I have heard.

This tendency to use people is particularly rife in ministry circles. When God gifts us with talented, willing people, it is amazingly easy to consume their talent on our vision and goals. After a while we begin to see them mainly as a means to an end, not as individuals with separate destinies, for which we should exercise responsible stewardship.

I belong to an organization called the International Reconciliation Coalition. One of our core values is that the function of a leader is to be a steward of the gifts of those he or she serves by using influence to promote them into their destiny. I have a dear friend who travels with me and serves me wholeheartedly. I enjoy her pleasant companionship. I could easily be tempted to spend her willingness and giftedness on my own needs and vision, but I want instead to seek to promote her into her own unique calling and destiny.

One of the main reasons there are so many church splits is a lack of proper stewardship of other people's gifts. If people have leadership gifts, do we as pastors seek to move them into their destiny or merely incorporate them into our own? If we would be intentional about leadership development focused on a person's destiny and calling, rather than on our own destiny and needs, we would see many more people come to Jesus.

HE EXPANDS OUR HEART
TO LOVE THE UNLOVELY

Catherine Booth, a vibrant woman who cofounded the Salvation Army with her husband, frequently visited prisons. One day as she entered a prison, she noticed a woman at the end of the corridor was violently resisting being put into a cell. Catherine immediately proceeded down the hall toward her. As she went she thought, *What can I do? Maybe I'll give her a Bible . . . no, she's too upset to read right now. Perhaps she might need some money . . . no, money will not help her.* Before Catherine had fully settled in her mind what she was going to do, she found herself face-to-face with the matted-haired young woman. Instinctively she kissed her on the cheek and then walked away.

The next day Catherine returned, and the warden told her she had to go visit that woman they had booked the previous day. She had kept asking, "Who was it that kissed me? Who was it that kissed me?" Catherine found her and asked gently, "Why do you ask?" The woman hesitantly replied, "When I was a baby my father left the family. We lived in a dank tenement basement, and my mother caught tuberculosis. When I was seven my mother died. But before she died, she took me in her arms and kissed me. *That was the last time before yesterday I knew anyone cared.*" Sometimes unlovely people are just one kiss away from God.

Because our weather in Southern California is so predictably warm, we tend to attract a large homeless population on our streets. When I was just learning to drive, I would be proudly tooling down the road with my mom. Often she would yell in commanding, no-uncertain-terms, "Stop!" My heart would race, wondering who I had just run over. She would leap out of the car, go up to someone singularly distasteful, reach in her purse, and pull out a little present. "Honey, I was praying I'd run into you. God told me to give you this." The person would break out into a great toothless smile. I knew it was most likely the first time in a long time that person had been honored by thoughtfulness. When Jesus is the heart of our relationships, He expands our hearts toward the unlovely.

Mother Teresa knew this fact. She saw Jesus in his "many distressing disguises" as she picked up maggot-eaten, half-dead bodies off the streets of Calcutta. When asked once by Senator Mark Hatfield how she stood the stress of continual need, she answered, "We are not called to be successful but to be obedient."

My friend, Harriet Weigel, spends her love and life on the disabled people of Ventura County. Daily she loves and prays for those who rarely appear on anyone else's radar. Harriet embraces the people the beautiful busy people dismiss. She relishes getting things in order to give them away. The only sure way to have Harriet keep something is to engrave her name on it. I remember one Thanksgiving, after Harriet had already distributed tons of food and love, someone gave her and her own disabled son a turkey and all the trimmings. She gave that away, as well, to some lonely elderly friends. She radiated joy when she recounted to me how much food she was able to distribute. Love oozes from every pore of this woman. You take one look at her face, and you want to know how Jesus could make anyone so beautiful.

When Jesus is the heart of our relationships, He expands our hearts to include others. John and Nancy Denhardter experience daily the heart-expanding love of Jesus in their servanthood to the underprivileged. John has told me extraordinary stories of the redemptive love of Jesus reaching out to abandoned children, to the hopelessly addicted, to the violent. One little boy was chained to a doghouse when his parents did not want to deal with him. Now Christians are caring for him, and he is vibrantly in love with Jesus. I speak at John's church several times a year and see with my own eyes the glory of Jesus on the faces of those who have fled to Him for refuge. They are stunning and beautiful, and their faces never fail to convict me of my perpetual mindlessness toward the poor.

HE EXPANDS OUR HEARTS
TO SPAN DIFFERENCES

A Hindu said to E. Stanley Jones one day, "You are such a broadminded Christian." He replied, "My brother, I am the narrowest man you have come across. I am broad on almost anything else, but on the one supreme necessity by the facts to one—Jesus . . . It is precisely because we believe in the absoluteness of Jesus that we can afford to take the more generous view of non-Christian systems and situations."[10]

I have found, over four decades of watching people, that the people who love Jesus most have the broadest hearts. Pride excludes, while love never loses an opportunity to include. Love always sets another place at the table. I have a dear friend who came out of the womb with a sword in her hand. She is militant, always ready to pick a fight with the enemy. If you were a demon, you'd be afraid to meet Marilyn Noorda in a dark alley. She is greatly respected and God has used her significantly to bring people together in California.

I, on the other hand, came out of the womb with a peace pipe. I rarely think in terms of wrestling with principalities and powers. I am a reconciler, who sees the absence of the glory of God a much greater concern than the presence of the demonic. And yet, we are friends, good friends. Because Jesus is the heart of our relationship, we love each other, pray for each other, and laugh at our huge differences of perspective and approach.

Sometimes in pastors' prayer gatherings there is dis-ease at each other's prayer styles. Usually the criticism falls into two categories: those who think the praying is too passionate and loud; and those who feel it is not passionate and loud enough. At one prayer summit, a group of pastors had a mini-summit in another chapel because they felt the larger group was just too conservative.

When we pray, we are addressing God, not each other. Who are we to say that we do not like how another person talks to God? It is not about us or our preferences. Prayer is all about Jesus. Can I critique how someone else relates to God? Am I even a part of the equation? Can we discover the heart of God while we exclude discovering the heart of our brothers and sisters? Obviously in prayer we must be sensitive to one another and take into account each other's culture. We have no one to exalt but Jesus and nothing to promote but prayer. Is Jesus really the heart of our relationships? Or do our cultural and doctrinal preferences in prayer take on a higher priority. Do we only want to be around people who are similar to us? Do we demonstrate His personality to each other through the fruits of the Spirit, no matter our differences? God made us to relish our diversity, recognizing that none of us can adequately express or understand the fullness and beauty of God by ourselves. Jesus enriches us with each other as He is the center, the heart of our friendships.

WE CALL OTHERS INTO
THEIR DESTINIES

God loves using us as mirrors for one another, reflecting not just what we are presently but what our friends are yet to become. Many years ago I enjoyed working with a talented young man on a worship team. The hand of the Lord was obviously upon Him. It took no discernment at all to notice. He moved to another city, and occasionally I would see him and ask if he was still doing music. No, he said he did not have time. He was now a schoolteacher, and if you have ever been a schoolteacher you know how much time teaching consumes. "But Scotty," I'd tell him, "you're supposed to be writing songs, leading worship, and making CDs." He'd smile graciously, knowing I loved him and was deeply prejudiced toward him. Now years later, much of the worldwide Body of Christ sings Scotty Underwood's worship music.

When I was young, a well-known songwriter at the time parted a crowd and told me I would be a writer someday. Her words lodged deep in my heart and gave me comfort, when it seemed no one would ever read a single thing I penned. Her confidence buoyed me as I dog-paddled for years through a sea of question marks about my destiny.

We see the power of this dynamic of calling things what are not as though they were when the angel of the Lord appears to Gideon, calling him a mighty man of valor. Gideon, at that very moment, was gallantly hiding behind a winepress trying to escape the detection of the

Midianites. He protested that God could not possibly use him because his father's family was poor; and to make matters even worse, he was the least in his father's household. It was not enough for Gideon to hear his future destiny from the Angel of the Lord. He needed to hear it from another person. And it just so happened it wasn't even a friend, but an enemy. Gideon overheard the Midianites talking about a dream they had about Gideon destroying them. Then he lead the charge, fully persuaded that he might be a deliverer after all.

None of us holds the key to ourselves. When Jesus is the heart of our friendships, He will expand our hearts. He will give us relationships that last. He will love the unlovely through us. He will enlarge our hearts to love people who were different than we are. He will keep us from using each other. He will give us the high privilege of unlocking each other into destiny. He does not call us servants; Jesus calls us friends.[12] And He bids us to call each other the same.

Seven

Jesus, the Heart of Our Story to Other Cultures

————

Christ . . . lifted with His pierced hands empires off their hinges and turned the stream of centuries out of its channel.[1]

—JEAN PAUL RICHTER

Many years ago an American was speaking to a crowd of people in Mexico and telling them the story of the Good Shepherd going after the lost lamb. Although he wasn't proficient in the language, he decided to preach in Spanish. He waxed eloquent, his arms waving as he told how the Good Shepherd leaves the ninety-nine and goes after the one lost lamb. He illustrated how the Shepherd finds the lamb, tenderly breaks its leg, and throws it over His shoulder so it will learn not to stray. To the evangelist's consternation, the more he spoke, the more his audience laughed. He saw tears in their eyes, but they were not the hoped-for tears of conviction. Finally someone was straight with him. In Spanish the word for *sheep* and the word for *old woman* are quite similar. He had been preaching about how the Good

Shepherd leaves the ninety-nine old women and goes to look for the one lost old woman. When He finds her, He takes the old woman, breaks her leg, and throws her over His shoulder. The man started using an interpreter.

While that true story is laughable, what is not is our confused use of the word *Christianity*, when we mean to speak of Christ. Confusing the two shows a woeful ignorance of history. Let me be the first to say that there have been bright and glorious moments of Christian history. But sadly, those moments have been few and often far between. God has always had a people who loved Him and loved others. There have always been those who in the meekness and humility of Jesus have poured out their lives to other cultures. Their lives are worthy of celebration and emulation. We should be swift to honor and celebrate the righteous history of God's people. But in talking about church as an institution, we must face some very hard facts.

Christ and *Christianity* are not synonymous. By using them to mean the same thing, we muck and blur the dazzling glory of Christ. When we say the word *Christianity* or the words *the Church* we often mean "The Body of Christ," or "lovers of Jesus." But for many indigenous peoples around the world, when you say *Christian*, you might as well be saying "arrogant, exploitative, culture-destroyers."

Christianity, not without reason, can often be the greatest hindrance to a culture's receiving the love of Christ. Confusing Christianity with Christ obscures the distinctive excellence of Jesus with the disastrous history of an institution. Just a quick read of church history will convince anyone the two are far from the same. Christ's innocent hands bled for His enemies, while Christianity's hands have often been stained with the innocent blood of others. Christ demonstrates by His life the power of love. Christianity often has demonstrated the love of power. Christ, in order to establish His Kingdom, sacrificed Himself. Christianity, in order to expand its kingdom, has often sacrificed its enemies.

I once gave a portfolio of old black-and-white pictures of New Delhi to a young friend from that city. They were very old pictures, and she looked at them with wonder. She told me she had never seen her city look like that. One was a picture of the university she attended. Another was of the temple where she celebrated her gods' birthdays. She said when the British left they gouged the precious stones out of the columns of the temples. This rape of architecture and the whole colonization of India, to many, represented not just Britain, but Christianity.

Of course, no one wants to dump all of British history in the lap of Christendom. Ghandi once said that, when he was young, all he thought Christianity meant was someone with brandy in one hand and beef in the other. He also said he loved their Christ but was not sure about their Christians.[2]

The associative collective memory of many cultures connects British colonization with Christianity. Given the history of Western imperialism, it is not hard to comprehend why exploited cultures around the world often wince and turn their head when they hear the word *Christianity*. But it is not just India that has a problem with Christianity.

Travel anywhere in the world and you will find a long history of exploitation, greed, and misrepresentation of the heart of God by self-professing Christians. Our history has often left a trail of blood along with tears. We must not forget that there have always been selfless people who have poured their lives out for indigenous cultures. We must study them, emulate them, and honor their memory. But the sad fact is they are rare.

What enabled the early church to turn the world upside down? Was it the propagation of Christianity or the proclamation of Christ? What was the one thing that Paul was determined to know—the person of Christ or a system of religious protocols and procedures?

CHRISTIANITY VERSUS CHRIST

The problem in discussing Christianity rather than Christ is that Christianity "began," as the late Richard Halverson noted, "as a fellowship around the person of Jesus Christ, went to Greece and became a philosophy, went to Rome and became an institution, went to Europe and became a culture, and came to America and became an enterprise."[3] It is a sad but true fact that Christianity is often the greatest deterrent to someone's discovering the marvelous person of Christ.

When Native Americans have experienced the ugliness of exploitation, greed, and selfishness, repeatedly done under the banner of Christianity, is it any wonder that they may be slow to accept Christ? When my husband, Joey, and I first went to the Philippines, I was shocked as

I listened to my Christian intellectual friends describe their hatred of America. I was shocked because I was ignorant of their history. I hadn't been in the country long enough to see the legitimacy of their claim that "Americans only come to become kings among the Orientals." We would talk long into the night, and I was slow of heart to comprehend.

One day my husband was on his way to visit a former head-hunting tribe in upper Luzon. He stopped to call on an American missionary in Manila. Joey was accompanied by two Swiss men and one Filipino. When the missionary opened the door, my husband and the Europeans were invited in, but the Filipino (who was a highly respected spiritual leader) was told to wait outside. When I heard this story my heart recoiled, and I began to understand. We had not come to other cultures as servants wanting to demonstrate the heart of God. We had come as colonizing and dominating spiritual authorities. My Filipino friends were right. We had become kings among the Orientals. We had not come to help escort the indigenous people to the thrones God had created for them to occupy. No, we had created our own empires under the guise of Christianity. We decided who and what was in and who was out. We jealously protected our territories. We were more invested in the institution of Christianity than we were committed to the liberating person of Jesus Christ.

When other cultures look at Christianity, it is not unfair for them to demand to see what it has produced in ours. Native American Indian Chief Red Jacket said in 1805:

"Brothers you say there is but one way to worship and serve the Great Spirit. If there is but one religion, why do you people differ so much about it? Why not all agree, as you can all read the same book . . . , Brothers, we are told you have been preaching to the white people in this place. These people are our neighbors. We are acquainted with them. We will wait a little while and see what effect your preaching has upon them. If we find it does them good, makes them honest, less disposed to cheat Indians, we will consider again of what you have said. Brothers, you have now heard our answer to your talk, and this is all we have to say at present. As we are going to part, we will come and take you by the hand, and hope the Great Spirit will protect you on your journey and return you safe to your friends."[4]

Sadly, we know exactly what Chief Red Jacket found. Preaching did not make us good or honest or less disposed to cheat Indians. If anything, we used Christianity as a rationale to deceive. The Indians are still waiting. We might be bewildered when other cultures do not readily embrace Christianity, but is it really Jesus they are rejecting? Missionary to India and author E. Stanley Jones comments on three glaring inconsistencies cemented into the formation of Western culture. These errors create powerful obstacles for other cultures to hear the claims of Jesus Christ.

Vladimir the Emperor of Russia desired to become a Christian but felt it was beneath his dignity to be baptized by a member of the local clergy. He thought it would be more fitting to be baptized by the Patriarch of Constantinople. But to ask the Patriarch to come would be acknowledging need. So he decided the appropriate thing to do was to conquer Constantinople and demand the Patriarch to baptize him. This is how Russia became Christian!

Charlemagne compelled the warring tribe of Europe, the Saxons, to become Christians. They agreed to baptism on one condition. They would not make that condition known until the time of their baptism. When the warriors were put under the water—they went in—all except for their right arms. They held them out, lifted above their heads. These were their fighting arms. No one who has been in Christendom long, will argue that fighting arms often still are sadly very much unbaptized.

The Mayflower that carried the Pilgrim Fathers went on her next trip for a load of slaves. The good ship "Jesus" was in the slave trade for our fathers. Race and color prejudice still exist today in the West, in spite of Christianity.[5]

Christianity and Jesus are not the same. We must make the distinction clear. We need to, as the apostle Paul says, "Preach Christ crucified."[6] As one author observes, "For in all the history of Christianity whenever there has been a new emphasis upon Jesus there has been a fresh outburst of spiritual vitality and virility."[7]

E. Stanley Jones' ministry to high-caste Brahmans, Hindus, and Mohammedans was freighted with Christ. He writes that when he first went to India he was trying to hold a very long line. The line stretched from Genesis to

Revelation, on to western civilization, and the western Church. He found himself bobbing up and down, fighting behind Moses and David and Jesus and Paul and western civilization and the Christian church. He was worried. There was no well-defined issue. He was always in a pitched battle trying to defend all three places. Instinctively he felt the heart of the matter was being left out. Jones decided to shorten his line and take his stand with Christ, and refuse before the non-Christian world to know anything save Jesus Christ and Him crucified.

He says, *"I saw that the gospel lies in the person of Jesus, that He himself is the Good News, that my one task was to live and to present him.* My task was simplified . . . not only was it simplified, it was vitalized. I found that when I was at the place of Jesus I was every moment upon the vital. He was the one question that settled all others."[8]

A Hindu lawyer once rose in one of E. Stanley Jones' meetings and said, "Do you mean to say that you are not here to wipe out our civilization and replace it with your own? Do you mean that your message is Christ without any implications that we must accept western civilization? I have hated Christianity, but if Christianity is Christ, I do not see how we Indians can hate it."[9]

When Jesus becomes the heart of our story, we find people engaged, attracted, and compelled to respond. Jesus said, "And I, if I am lifted up from the earth, will draw all peoples to Myself."[10] Could it be that our lack of success in proclaiming Christianity to other cultures is that Jesus often is only one aspect of our message, not *the* message? I grew up in churches that prided themselves not on Jesus, but on *what they did not do*. I remember coming home from high school one day and saying, "Mom, I met the sweetest girl at school today. She's a Christian! But, Mom," I said in a hushed, gossipy whisper, *"she wears pants."* I was genuinely puzzled that someone could love God and wear pants!

Could a Maori love God, paint his face, and do the Haka? Can a Native American love God and worship Him in regalia, beating a drum? If the heart of our story is Jesus, and not a particular cultural tradition or doctrinal position, the answer is of course quite open and embracing. When Jesus is the heart of all we proclaim, our basis of relationship is Jesus, and Jesus alone. By making Jesus central, we eradicate the high walls of "us and them" endemic to the human condition.

Our culture, our traditions, our personal preferences, and our personality have been inseparably intertwined with the message of Jesus. Other cultures recoil in self-protection. Are we trying to turn hearts to Jesus, or to turn people into our version of acceptable culture? Is there really a specific "look" that is more holy, more acceptable to God than others? What do we want other cultures and generations to do? What's our dream for them to become? Do we enjoy their distinctive thoughts and practices? Are we aware of how inadequate we are apart from them? Or do we subtly judge them . . . comparing our culture with theirs? Is Jesus really the heart of our story?

Richard Twiss, a Lakota/Sioux reconciliation leader, convenes Many Nations—One Voice worship gatherings of indigenous peoples from all over the world. As the nations and tribes come in stunning regalia to lay their offerings at the cross, it is hard not to weep for the worthiness of the Lamb. What a contrast to the pale, boring, watercolor vision I have had of heaven! In light of the beauty of the worldwide bride, how pitiful it is to be ethnocentric in our worship. Imagine worshiping with the passion of the Irish, the humility of the Peruvians, the creativity and humor of the Native Americans, the dignity of the Africans. What kind of God can command such extravagant worship from every tribe and tongue? Isn't the fact that God elicits such passionate worship from so many different cultures a testimony to the fact that He is indeed God? Because Jesus is all we proclaim to other cultures, we allow those cultures to offer themselves as they are, freely and completely to Him. Being in the presence of Jesus with our brothers and sisters from other cultures widens the borders of our being. Just as our bodies are made up of many parts, and would be incomplete without the diversity of different organs, so we can never be complete in the Body of Christ apart from other cultures. When He is our focus, our eyes fix on Him and we see each other with startling clarity—and know we are rich beyond telling.

When Jesus is the heart of our story, our cultural differences become irrelevant. I have been privileged to pray and worship with brothers and sisters from many different cultures and perspectives. As we pray together Jesus becomes luminous. We come to understand we each *belong* to Him. As we treasure Him we prize each other. E. Stanley Jones records,

As the wedding processions go through the streets of an Indian city at night, the torch bearers will hold up their torches so that the bridegroom, seated on his bedecked horse is illuminated. Christ said of the Holy Spirit, "He shall glorify me"-He makes luminous the person of Christ, and because Christ is central and luminous, marginal differences no longer command the situation.[11]

LEARNING TO DISCERN THE HOLY FROM THE PROFANE

Do we trust that other cultures can come to their own conclusions about extracting what is holy from what is profane under the loving gaze of Jesus? Will Jesus be faithful to the Maori, the Irish, the Jews, the American Indians, the Sammi of Norway, and all indigenous believers, faultless before God's throne? Do we trust the Holy Spirit? Jacob prophesies, "to Him shall be the obedience of the people."[12] When we treasure our brothers and sisters from other cultures, we realize that the same Holy Spirit who produces obedience in us is faithful to guide them.

When Bruce Olsen went to the Motilone tribe in South America, he did not see one person converted for six years. Then Kobuayrd Bobarishora (Bobby) came to trust Jesus. Bruce urged him to testify of his newfound faith to the rest of the tribe. But Bobby waited. In Motilone culture, news has no significance unless it's given in a formal ceremony.

Then one day there was a Festival of Arrows. It was the only gathering where all the Motilones came together.

They traded arrows, made pacts, and had a singing contest. An older chief challenged Bobby to a song. They climbed into a single hammock twenty feet off the ground, and Bobby began to sing about how the Motilones had lost God's trail. Then he began to sing about Jesus. The other men who were singing in their own contests stopped and listened. For fourteen hours the two men laid in their hammock singing. Bruce was covering his ears, thinking, *I cannot believe he's doing this, this is witch music.* The song was chanted in a strange minor key. As the chanting continued Bruce realized the only evil thing happening was his own heart attitude. Even though Bruce loved the Motilone way of life, he felt superior when it came to spiritual matters. The chief, at the end, said, "You've communicated a true news item. I too want to suspend myself in Jesus. I want to pull His blood over my deception." That night the whole tribe was buzzing with talk of Jesus. Everyone wanted Him to take them over the horizon. Bruce Olsen learned at that moment the utter trustworthiness of the Holy Spirit.[13]

When other cultures express their faith in contexts that are unfamiliar to us, can we trust the Holy Spirit to fulfill His job description of leading and guiding into all truth? Must we usurp the Holy Spirit and exalt our opinions as ultimate guide to what is holy and pure? Could we relax in the realization that Jesus will present all of us faultless before the presence of His glory with joy?

One of the advantages of age is being able to see the long view of movements. As I have observed the Body of Christ over the last forty years, I have seen many things certain segments of the Body of Christ were at one time adamantly against, now simply standard practice. No one even bats an eye. Things like drums, expressive worship, modern Bible translations, make-up, television. In the old days, if it was new, it was suspect. If we allow ourselves the grace to change our perspective over time, can we extend that same grace to other cultures?

OUR FEAR OF THE UNFAMILIAR GREATER THAN OUR LOVE

Could our fear of the unfamiliar be greater than our love for Christ and for those He loves? Recently I drove into Los Angeles International Airport to drop off some friends. I thought to myself how much I disliked the city. Clogged traffic, poor air quality, lack of cohesive aesthetic, weak city planning, it all made me wrinkle up my nose and long for the beauty of home an hour north. Immediately I heard the still, small voice of the Holy Spirit say: *But there are millions of people here made in His image. You love Him, don't you?* I was speechless with conviction that I had just insulted God by dismissing people He passionately loves. I was quick to repent. Moments later, I reveled in the diversity of Orthodox Jews, Islanders, Africans, and Orientals waiting for a plane together. When Jesus is the heart of our story, even our geographical preferences no longer dictate our loves.

The best way for people to become world Christians is for them to become white-hot lovers of Jesus. When we love Him, we love what He loves. When we love Jesus, He enlarges our hearts. He takes an American named Adoniram Judson, sends him to Burma, and causes him to fall in love with the Burmese and their culture. He takes British-born Hudson Taylor and allows his heart to so love the Chinese that he wears the pigtail and silks of a Chinese teacher. He takes a man like E. Stanley Jones and enlarges his heart in such a way that he becomes an adopted son of India. Jones was so broadened by the love of God that complex India found in his heart a spacious and loved home.

The Moravians, overcome by the love of Christ, sold themselves into slavery in order to share the love of Christ with African slaves in the West Indies. Ravi Zacharias told the story at Amsterdam 2000 of Belgian priest Father Damien who went to the lepers of Moloki in Hawaii. He loved them passionately and did not even realize he had become a leper until he dropped some hot water on his foot and realized he did not feel any pain. He purposely dropped some more on his other foot and again felt nothing. That Sunday he mounted the pulpit and said "My brothers, we lepers . . ." When he finally died, the government of Holland wanted his body. The lepers pled that part of his body be buried on Moloki. Their request was granted. Damien's heart and one arm lies buried in their soil.

White-hot lovers of Jesus often do radical things with their lives. My husband and I once served a Lebanese woman who loved the prisoners of New Bilibid prison in the Philippines. It was, at that time, the largest prison in the world. The prisoners loved her to such an extent that they built her a house on the prison grounds. She was completely at home in maximum security and on death row. They called her "Mamma."

But her life there was not all sweetness and joy. Once a prisoner hid in her van as she was leaving the prison, holding a knife to the throat of one of her passengers. She slammed on the brakes at the exit of the prison, swung open the door, and leapt out while the van kept rolling. High impact bullets pockmarked the van as the guards blew off the face of the fugitive. What gives an older single woman the grace to live in a foreign nation and make her home in the midst of hardened criminals? Only the love of Jesus. Only for love of Jesus can God take someone like Olga, enlarge her heart for prisoners, and fulfill her as a mother to nine thousand Filipino men.

He may take you, dear reader, and send you to a segment of society that has never even made an appearance on your radar screen. You might end up loving them, perhaps even becoming an adopted son or daughter of that culture. Because Jesus is the heart of our story, we are honored to love those He loves. We are free to enjoy each culture's unique expression of who God is. We are enriched and enlarged to savor and delight in the qualities of Jesus hidden in every culture. Our message becomes invincible, because Jesus is invincible. When Jesus is the heart of our story to other cultures, we tell an irresistible story of an irresistible Christ. Because Jesus is all we proclaim, we have no one else to promote, no doctrine to protect, no protocol to preserve. It's really all about Him.

Eight

Jesus, the Heart of Our Story to a New Generation

Every one of us is something the other is not, and there-fore knows something—it may be without knowing that he knows it—which no one else knows. It is everyone's business as one of the kingdom of light and inheritor in it all, to give his portion to the rest.[1]

—GEORGE MACDONALD

Strikingly handsome, tattoos sprawl over his skin like gangs loose on a graffiti spree. Tiny silver rings pierce his skin. He is artsy, on the edge. When I look into the eyes of this vision-satiated young man, Jesus unflinchingly looks back at me—clean, pure, entirely unashamed. The favor of God hovers over his life like a billboard. I do not need a lick of discernment to read it. God's touch is that obvious.

Of course, I *could* clutch my self-righteous robes around me, excluding my brother because his culture is foreign to mine. If I did however, I would be the poorer. Were I to casually dismiss him, I would deprive myself of a major clue to the treasure that is Jesus. Jesus is what Greg and I have in common. And in Jesus, we share a whole universe beyond all worlds and traditions. Because Jesus is our shared passion, nothing else really needs to be. Musical taste, generational protocol, dress, art. What does it matter?

Only twice in my life have people come up to me and asked me what to do with money they wanted to invest in ministry. The first time, the question came from a prosperous businessman I did not know. He came to me and said he wanted to help young people. What should he do with his money? I said, "Give it to Greg to buy that theatre downtown. He's the best investment you can make. He'll fill it with a generation of kids hungry for God." I never heard from that man again, but I applaud his desire to invest in young people. God is raising up a whole tribe of people willing to invest in this generation. Imagine the possibilities if we poured our time, treasure, and talent into this present generation of Jesus lovers! When all is said and done, we actually only have two choices—pour ourselves into maintaining the status quo or pour our lives into blessing the future. Every generation is offered the same choice.

JESUS, THE HEART ENLARGER

When Jesus is the heart of our story, He starts producing stretch marks as He enlarges the borders of our being. He gently encourages us to embrace what seems foreign. He broadens our scope. He enlarges our radar screens and causes us to care about people we once easily dismissed. We find ourselves with ever-expanding interests and passions.

Eugene Peterson talks about the birthing potential of a fertile heart.

> Self-love is barren, infertile. Love is fertile. Self-love is attached to the familiar, the cozy: possessions, customs. Love is detached from the cloying clutter and therefore open to fertilization by the new, open to the ecstasy of intercourse and the act of creation. Attachment is closed up and walled in. Detachment opens out and grows up.[2]

I am increasingly finding God's pleasure as I embrace and enjoy this new generation, which has taken me completely by surprise. It is one of those God-moves I could not have planned and certainly did not anticipate. I was born forty. I have always felt most comfortable with forty-somethings. But now I find myself increasingly speaking to audiences of seventeen to twenty-four-year-olds. I find them open, hungry for spiritual parenting, craving God. God is actively turning my heart like a large sailboat readjusting its tack, racing into this generation.

Recently I received a call from a young YWAM leader who is conducting prayer and revival schools across California. John had read my first book, *Honor*, and was calling to say that God had given him a vision to build a bridge of honor between my generation and the new generation.

As I listened to this young man's vision, I felt awash in holy possibilities. Can you see spiritual mothers and fathers wrapping their arms around this generation, praying them into their destinies? Can you see fathers in the faith joining with mothers in Israel, lavishing their natural and spiritual inheritance on this generation? Can you see my generation reenlisting in the purposes of God, pledging themselves to serve this generation? Will God fulfill Malachi 4:6 in our time? Is this the hour that He will turn the hearts of the fathers to their sons, the hearts of the parents toward their young? Are you possibly, dear reader, someone God is summoning to bless this generation into its high and holy destiny?

When Jesus is our treasure, we will bridge culture, generations, and traditions—anything—to get to Him and to bring others with us. Can you picture a generation of Jesus lovers, nameless and faceless, desiring nothing more than for the renown and fame of Jesus to cover the earth? Can you imagine a revival that does not fizzle out after a few years but lasts for decades, a revival of a passion for Jesus? It may be now simply a cloud the size of a man's hand but I believe it could become the perfect storm. This may very well be the generation of those who seek Him.

God is doing an extraordinary thing. We are sitting in front-row seats cheering the Holy Spirit, eagerly watching Him stir this generation. Children, teens, and young adults across the globe are praying not "now-I-lay-me-down-to-sleep" prayers, but prayers that rock cities and nations. They are reminding us that Jesus in a child or teenager is just as fully Himself as He is in an adult. He does not reduce Himself by an inch because of age. Little children do not have a junior Holy Spirit. Religious ideas or phrases do not clutter their prayers. My church recently had children as the prayer team during the Sunday morning service. They were stationed around the auditorium during worship. I rushed down from the balcony and asked a beautiful African-American child to pray over this book and another that I was writing. "Lord Jesus, make it easy," Destiny prayed fervently. Now that was a prayer I could whole-heartedly agree with!

I have spoken in meetings in which young, college-age kids were weeping on their faces, pleading with God to have mercy on their generation. This stunning posture is not just happening in isolated areas, it is happening all over the world. England has been a catalyst for a growing youth movement praying twenty-four hours a day, seven days a week, across the nations. This is not your father's prayer meeting. They plaster butcher paper on the walls so they can write poetry or draw pictures. There are candles, sometimes incense. They accommodate many different prayer styles and personalities. Some pace, some kneel. They record their prayers on the Internet for a worldwide audience of like-minded youth. They are imploring God with strong passion to capture this generation for Jesus. Here is a glimpse of the passion of Pete Grieg:

> So this guy comes up to me and says, "What's the vision? What's the big idea?" I open my mouth and words come out like this: The vision? The vision is *Jesus*! Obsessively, dangerously, undeniably Jesus . . . It's an army of young people. They laugh at 9-5 little prisons. They could eat caviar on Monday and crusts on Tuesday. They wouldn't

even notice. They are mobile like the wind; they belong to the nations. They need no passport . . . They are free yet they are slaves of the hurting and dirty and dying. What is the vision? The vision is holiness that hurts the eyes. It makes children laugh and adults angry. It gave up the game of minimum integrity long ago to reach for the stars. It scorns the good and strains for the best. It is dangerously pure. Light flickers from every secret motive, every private conversation. It loves people away from their suicide leaps; their Satan games . . . They do not need fame from names. Instead they grin quietly upwards and hear the crowds chanting again and again: "COME ON!" . . . The tattoo on their back boasts "for me to live is Christ and to die is gain." Winners. Martyrs.

Who can stop them? Can hormones hold them back? Can failure succeed? Can fear scare them or death kill them? And the generation prays like a dying man with groans beyond talking, with warrior cries, sulfuric tears and with great barrow loads of laughter! Whatever it takes they will give: Breaking the rules. Shaking mediocrity from its cozy little hide. Laying down their rights and their precious little wrongs, laughing at labels, fasting essentials. The advertisers cannot mold them. Hollywood cannot hold them. Peer pressure is powerless to shake their resolve at late night parties before the cockerel cries.[3]

Does that sound hopelessly naïve? Does cynicism whisper its self-authenticating doubt in your ear? Could God take really take a generation orphaned in Spirit and use them to shake the earth? I believe the years to come will shout a resounding, "Yes!" Kirk Dewitt, a pastor friend, asked a couple of young artists to design an advertising campaign for a new postmodern service that he was starting. He was startled when they returned their work. It was simply a painting of the face of Jesus. No words, no catchy slogans or jingles. Just the face of Jesus. My friend spent a couple of days with the picture. He blew it up; he shrunk it down; he slowly realized it was the perfect description of what they were about as a congregation. Just Jesus. Not Jesus plus anything.

I believe this "It's All About You, Jesus" emphasis is one of the premier gifts of this generation. Jesus alone is their consuming passion. Personality worship, no matter how gifted or anointed the personality, will become odious. God is raising up a generation that will not pledge their loyalty and commitment to institutions and organizations. No longer will entertainment and pleasure seduce us. "When they had lifted up their eyes, they saw no one but Jesus only."[4] Jesus, and Jesus alone, will be the preeminent One in our thinking, in our speaking, in our gatherings, in our cosmology.

Francis Frangipane writes,

> The world and all it contains was created for one purpose: to showcase the grandeur of God's Son. In Jesus, the nature of God is magnificently and perfectly revealed; He is the expressed image of God, the fullness of the Godhead in bodily form.[5]

Last week I mailed an invitation to pastors and leaders about an upcoming countywide Concert of Prayer. I smiled to myself as we prepared it. My generation has to see prominent names on stationery. The signature of a convening power-pastor often defines if an event is worthy of attendance. That is why it is wise to have a board of reference that reads like a spiritual *Who's Who*. My generation feels secure if someone they respect in pastoral ministry endorses an event. But that is not how the new generation thinks at all. Names do not matter. They do not even tell you half the time who the speaker is or who the band will be! They are saying, "Come for Jesus! Come because God is summoning you! Come because it's all about Jesus!"

Recently at a gathering called Oneday, 30,000 young adults from eighteen to twenty-five years of age gathered at Shelby Farms in Tennessee to seek God and worship. When asked who the bands and speakers were going to be, the promoters gave this answer:

> Our greatest challenge has been to keep the main thing front and center. OneDay is, in its purest sense; a day set aside for prayer and worship before God. It's not about people, famous or otherwise. One way to keep our purpose in view is to remove attention from the people God has chosen to lead us. They are coming not because they will sing or speak, but because of their desire to kneel before Him on this day. You will know and appreciate them, *but come for Jesus. He's the center around whom we gather.*

This emphasis on Jesus and de-emphasis on people is another premiere gift of this emerging generation. One young girl in Texas saw a vision of herself carrying a large cross over her shoulder. As she walked the cross erased her footprints. This is a potent visual metaphor of the future. God is forming a nameless, faceless, selfless generation who will not name ministries and universities after themselves. They will not build empires around their anointing. They will not erect tollbooths to collect money as you cross their particular bridge into your future in God. This single-eyed passion is beginning to rub off on my generation. Just last night I noticed an advertisement for a Solemn Assembly, a fifty-hour interracial gathering of Pentecostals. This group has repented for the racial divide that split the Pentecostal movement at the turn of the century. They, too, while having prominent well-known speakers, are choosing not to list who they are or when they'll speak.

GENERATIONAL BRIDGES

God is looking for Calebs who will span the generations with the goodness of God on their lips. We either choose to be Caleb, or we die with the rest on the plains of unbelief. We can embrace God's promise for the future or try to preserve our sacrosanct routines. I was reminded of this fact recently in a prayer gathering.

They came in quietly and sat in the back rows. I wondered quietly if perhaps everyone in their church was the same age. Most of them seemed to be in their seventies. I was thrilled. Ah, yes, these are the people God tells us to honor. We are to stand in the presence of gray hairs. They were here for a multichurch Concert of Prayer. Since my church is composed of thousands of people under forty, I am always on the lookout for mothers and fathers in Israel. Here they were, all neatly lined up in the back rows, fairly brimming with history in God.

But when I looked more carefully, I saw a tenuous hesitancy surrounding them. They appeared uncomfortable in a church different from their own. They withdrew, not reaching out to the rest of us. I wondered about their story. Had my generation scorned them? Had we despised them and forced them into isolation? Had they despised us? The new, the different, the generation that did not know hymns, that had the attention spans of gnats and no tolerance for long sermons? Had they written us off because we were easily bored?

We eyed each other across wide generational chasms. My heart ached for what could have been. Missed opportunities for mentoring another generation in the ways and heart of God. We had sinned in not valuing their experience. They had sinned in not passing on the baton to a new generation. We had not prayed for each other and opened our arms.

I looked at them and realized that I unreasonably longed for their embrace. In my mid-forties I knew as well that another generation was looking at me with the same unexpressed longings. And so it would be, generation after generation, either rejecting or embracing one another. Either speaking life and encouragement or speaking disdain. We would either open our arms to embrace or point our fingers to accuse. The pointed-finger crowd would spend their lives clustered in holy little huddles making cozy their nest, keeping out intruders who did not fit. The embracers would be forever on the grow, tearing apart the nests of old paradigms, casting to the wind little fledglings, swooping down under them with joy, like a mother eagle swoops under her young.

The pointed-finger crowd will fortress themselves behind the flag of self-preservation. They will watch with vigilant wariness any aberration, anything suspect of true holiness. They would rather raise an eyebrow of suspicion than joyfully applaud God's wild, reckless mercy.

BUSY COPY EDITORS
OR AVID LISTENERS

Do we love Jesus so much that, if He is the heart of the story, we will listen to any tale, no matter who is telling it? I have friends who said to their denomination, "Look, we are about to retire. We have pastored some great churches; we do not have anything to prove. Assign us your deadest church. If God does not turn it around, it's no skin off our egos. If He does do a work there [and they believed He would], it is all the more glory for God." Their denomination sent them to a church where death circled like a vulture awaiting the final breath of its prey.

My friends prayed passionately and loved intensely; and God started (as He usually will with those two ingredients) doing a work. Motorcycle gang members started getting saved. They would ask for weddings to be performed after the service, convicted by the Holy Spirit of living together. During one service a burly man went to an open mike and said, *"The presence of God is so in this place, my tits are hard!"* Could we laugh with joy upon hearing that someone was experiencing the presence of God, or would we draw back in judgment that someone mentioned a body part that is not usually brought up in polite company?

Author, thinker, lover of God, Eugene Peterson comments:

> The self is persistent, quietly, subtly, ingeniously, it works itself back to center . . . we have, unawares, become officious clerks in the house of creation, concerned with neatness of the bookkeeping but oblivious to the wild and extravagant exchanges of mercy and grace that take place all around us as God speaks. We become busybody copy editors to the people around us who are learning to tell the story of God's saving love in their lives: we delete commas, rearrange semicolons, get cranky with the sloppiness of the story that they tell in their breathless but awkward syntax.[7]

Do we love Jesus enough to applaud His grace in any life, to welcome with itching ears His story, no matter how it is spoken, where the plot begins, or who the characters are? Are we really all about Him, or are we "I" specialists?

A GENERATIONAL STATEMENT
OF REPENTANCE

Recently fourteen young seventeen- to twenty-four-year-olds from different states came to my house for a day. We sat together in the presence of Jesus, ate together, and listened to each other's stories. I shared with them a statement of repentance[8] from my generation I had written for them the night before.

I said that God's holy ambition for them was to be loved and cherished by godly parents, I confessed my generation's self-centeredness, self-absorption, and self-preoccupation. We had worshiped at the altar of our own fulfillment, prizing pleasure and putting our standard of living, our careers, above their right to live and be nourished with tender, emotionally present parents.

We had sacrificed forty million of them on the altar of convenience. Those who survived the womb were relegated to daycare, schools, babysitters, and entertainment. We did not accept the sacred privilege of mentoring them and calling them into their destiny of loving and knowing God.

Because all sin is a sin against relationship, we had sinned in not modeling loyalty in our marriages and commitments. We had failed to demonstrate through our relationships the unconditional love and loyalty of God. I said that God's intent was that His heart would be known by how we loved and cherished them. But my generation had birthed an entire generation orphaned in spirit. The roots and tendrils of rejection festered deep in the core of their being. We had abdicated our God-given role in their lives.

In churches we had been visionless with their education. We merely baby-sat, when we could have ushered them into their destiny. We could have helped them discover their gifts. We could have introduced them to the power of the Holy Spirit, but we settled instead for the power of entertainment. We popped in videos instead of pouring out our lives.

I said we wanted the fruit of our repentance to be proved in giving our influence to them, in sharing our resources, blessing and empowering them with our prayers, enfolding them in our love and embrace. We needed their forgiveness. They tearfully extended it to me and asked for my forgiveness that their generation had not honored us. They repented for rebellion and for exploiting my generation's failures. We tearfully embraced each other in trusting God to redeem our sin. It was a holy, somber moment, a space in time where two generations peer into their history through the eyes of God and weep.

I was asked later to read this declaration of repentance at a youth conference. I asked everyone forty years and older to come stand with me as I read. Crying began to mount as I read the long list of our sins. I did not have glasses on at the time, and so I read slowly, carefully, wanting to give the moment a sobriety worthy of repentance. I became aware it was the adults that were weeping. I was articulating their sorrow. They were speaking their repentance along with me in tears.

GETTING TO KNOW THIS GENERATION

I am by nature fairly contemplative. I do not like loud music or wailing, whiny guitars. My preferred worship music is quiet, gentle, and intimate. But if you come to my house unexpectedly, the walls might be convulsing with pulsating rhythms. I listen to this generation's worship music because it gives me a glimpse of their heart. And I love what I see. The worship is passionate; it's highly Jesus-focused; it's worship that's willing to die for the One it loves. Clues abound in every song to what God has woven into this generation.

If we allow Jesus to give us His heart for this generation, we will seek to understand how they think. What makes them unique? How do they hear? How has media impacted their learning style? This generation listens with their eyes and thinks with their feelings. Like all humans, they can hold contradictory beliefs together without tension. That is the reality of their lives and background. I cannot authentically love them without seeking to understand their distinctive traits. When Jesus is the heart of our story, we have nothing to preserve of our own preferences. His interests, His loves become our own.

Will we be put off by their differences, or will we rush to embrace them? Will we make them become like we are or encourage them to be like Jesus? Will we make a pilgrimage into the purposes of God together, arm in arm, relishing the holy reciprocity God intended between generations? I believe the Holy Spirit is insistent that there truly is no other way. Each new generation should build its foundation on the rooftop of the past generation's experience with God.

BUY THE FIELD

Jeremiah sobs repeated warnings to Israel that God has judged them, and that they will be removed off their land and taken captive by the Babylonians. We now know that that captivity lasted seventy years. But in the midst of these repeated warnings, the Lord instructs Jeremiah to do a very curious thing. While he is in jail for his prophecy, he buys the field of a local relative and seals up the deed in a clay jar. It made as much sense as buying land next to Chernobyl after the meltdown. But God had Jeremiah close this ridiculous escrow because He intended to underscore a vital point. We must be invested in the goodness of God for the next generation. Instead of cowering in fear at present judgment, we must have confident expectancy in the future goodness of God. We must spend our obedience, our resources on providing land we may never see for a new generation.

When I visit places like Yosemite National Park my heart fills with gratitude to think that people set aside land for future generations to enjoy. The park system in the United States has been preserved by forward-thinking people who knew that beauty was not to be squandered, not to be exploited for personal gain. We too can preserve for the next generation not just stunning geography, but maps to the astonishing wonder of God's heart. We haven't a second to lose. Find a way to begin today.

Nine

Jesus, the Heart of Our Mentoring

Jesus as the actual teacher of His people has disappeared from the mental horizon of our faith. In that capacity he is not part of how we "do" our Christianity today. It is a main purpose of this book to help us face this fact of the absence of Jesus the teacher and to change it.[1]

—DALLAS WILLARD

When Jesus was asked where He lived, He did not give an address. He issued a friendly invitation, "Come, see!" And He's been saying that to each apprentice ever since. John the Apostle writes later in his life, "That which was from the beginning, which we have heard, which we have seen with our eyes, which we have looked upon, and our hands have handled, concerning the Word of life—the life was manifested, and we have seen, and bear witness."[2] Jesus' curriculum was almost exclusively field trips. He wanted His apprentices to see Him in action. It will come as no surprise to a visual generation but may be a shock to an older, auditory generation that God uses the word *see* more often than the word *hear*. God understood all along what we are now just discovering. We learn more by watching than by hearing, which leads one to ask, how many other startling new discoveries are hidden in the Word in plain sight for the careful observer?

Unfortunately the church has embraced and excelled in the auditory over all other possible ways of learning. "Come hear so-and-so preach!" Even our attempts at visual media are really mostly an auditory affair. When we mentor, we generally seek to fill ears with words rather than eyes with visions. Paul said, "And my speech and my preaching were not with persuasive words of human wisdom, but in demonstration of the Spirit and of power, that your faith should not be in the wisdom of men but in the power of God."[3] Study Jesus as mentor, and you find He mentors by demonstration instead of information. Look at Jesus mentor His apprentices and new possibilities enlarge your heart in discipleship.

MENTORED BY HIS PRESENCE

Jesus mentored His apprentices with His presence, up close and personal. Jesus was not only the disciples' subject, He was their classroom, their text. He never sat them down in a room to study Torah by themselves—no distance learning, no independent study in His school. Jesus did not give credits for "life experience" or even accept transfer credits from other institutions. The disciples did not have guest lecturers who supplemented the course material. Jesus was their theme, spelled out before them in action, larger than life, 24/7/365 for three staggering years.

The Bible says, "He called His disciples to Himself,"[4] and with Him they were, as He pulled off jaw-dropping miracles. They wiped their mouths with the crowd as Jesus fed thousands with a joyful meal. Their ears were scandalized as Jesus tenderly responded to the woman with the issue of blood. They had front-row seats as He fleshed out the kingdom of God bending their ears with riveting stories. They slunk back in fright as demons drooled and foamed and gagged confession of His Lordship. They were there almost every moment, clueless as to what might come next. They were *with* Him. In fact the very finest complement ever given to the disciples was, "Now when they saw the boldness of Peter and John, and perceived that they were uneducated and untrained men, they marveled. And they realized that they had been with Jesus."[5]

Jesus' approach somehow got lost in how we now do discipleship. As Westerners, our culture's greatest gift is also our greatest occupational hazard. We excel in quantifiable productivity. We prize measurable activity over every other thing, particularly relationship. While we are marvelous at getting things done, we are weak in creating passionate apprentices of Jesus. We think we can impart life through books and quizzes.

We calculate spirituality by grade point averages. We send people off to the classroom, load them up with a bunch of texts, and drill them on how many facts they can remember. We stuff them full of irrelevant information that has little to do with knowing God. Karl Barth once said, "The Word become flesh—and then through theologians it became words again."[6] We stuff heads, not hearts.

Little of what I learned in Bible college had real-life consequences or drew me closer to God. If anything, my education distanced and deadened me to God's life-giving Word. Even though I attended a very conservative school, I came close to losing my faith. In scrutinizing texts with a fine-tooth comb and speculating, *Is this verse an interpolation or not?* I almost lost Jesus in the very thicket of His Word. Do our students leave our classrooms deeper friends with Jesus? Are their heads pumped with facts or are their hearts ablaze with love? Is Jesus truly the heart of our mentoring? An hour in the presence of Jesus will teach you more about Him than a decade of academic research. Will those we are mentoring today be in passionate pursuit of Jesus tomorrow?

Discipleship was never meant to be an academic affair. It is an ongoing, deepening relationship with Jesus. And it is more than a just a relationship. It is a journey, a pilgrimage *into* the very life of Jesus. We are not understudies; we become a part of Him. We do not ask, "What would Jesus do?" as though He is some historical figure and we need to remember how He might have responded. We ask, "What is Jesus doing? What is He saying? How at this very moment is He living His life in me?" Our union with Him is our only wisdom.

I once had breakfast with a young man who was being mentored by Paul Eschleman of the Jesus Film Project. It turned out that the two of us were alumni of the same college on the East Coast. I remarked what a great college it was, how it had a fine reputation. To my amazement, this handsome young man vehemently disagreed. He was very articulate and passionate that the fruit in his life from being mentored by Paul Eshleman far exceeded anything he ever gained at college. He said he wished for every young man a spiritual father who truly knew God. I was taken aback at how adamant he was. In the years since that conversation, I have realized the truth of his words. Besides being continually in the presence of Jesus, being consistently in the presence of a godly man or woman is the most soul enriching, heart expanding environment possible.

Impartational Versus Informational

Those who powerfully mentor others are impartational rather than informational. Moses was instructed by God to impart his anointing and authority to Joshua. In Numbers 27:18–20 we read: "And the Lord said to Moses: 'Take Joshua the son of Nun with you, a man in whom is the Spirit, and lay your hand on him . . . and inaugurate him in their sight. And you shall give . . . your authority to him, that all the congregation of the children of Israel may be obedient.'"

There is power in understanding that we each have something we can bestow or grant to others. The gifts and callings God gives us were never intended to be one-act plays, one-person monologues of ministry. God's gifts are shareware. God imparts to us, and we impart to others. It's like God hands us valentines to hand out to others from Him. It is important to identify specifically what you have been given by God to impart.

Much to my dismay, I have found after I pray for people they seem to always want to take a nap. They feel as if they have been soaking in a Jacuzzi. How dynamic is that? When many of my friends pray for you, you want to go set the world on fire with passion for Jesus; and when I pray for you, you will most likely want to find a quiet spot and drool on your pillow. I was extremely disappointed when I saw this consistently happen to those with whom I prayed. All I seemed to have to impart was peace. Finally it dawned on me that there happen to be a lot of people who actually need peace. I was in an emergency room for many hours the other night, and I realized I could walk around quietly, smile a lot, and bestow peace, everywhere I looked. I recently was with a friend who travels and speaks widely. We were in a very open café and began praying impartational prayers for each other. This person is highly gifted, and I thought self-consciously and with a tinge of regret, *All I have to impart is peace, and I doubt she needs peace.* We were very observable, so I kept my eyes glued shut, much like little children who think you cannot see them if they close their eyes. When I finally got brave enough to open my eyes, my friend had tears flowing down her face. God had touched her. Peace, it turned out, was *exactly* what she needed. Never underestimate what God has given you to impart to others, even if you think it's low on the food chain of desirable gifts.

CHRIST OR CLONES

Just as there is usually a family resemblance in our children, we produce who we are spiritually. If we are the intellectual-inquiring-minds-want-to-know type, chances are that those we mentor will be the same. We enjoy people who are like we are. We mentor people after our image and likeness. Much of our mentoring is centered on trying to create people who will toe the company line. We want people to wear our logo, speak our lingo, and believe our mission statement. We want people to like what we like and dislike what we loathe. We can make people who do all the right things and observe all the traditional taboos of our respective traditions, but whose character may not reflect Jesus in the slightest. Mentoring new believers is not a process of casting them in our image but allowing who Jesus actually is to become integrated into who they actually are.

Richard Twiss, a Lakota/Sioux reconciliation leader, early in his Christian life cut his hair, wore three-piece suits, and sported wing-tip shoes, imagining he had to become a white man to please God. He was taught that being godly meant the negation of who he was. Today Richard wears the stunning regalia of a Lakota/Sioux warrior and holds Many Nations–One Voice conferences, where cultures from all over the world worship Jesus with their own traditional gifts. Jesus never negates; He fully enhances who we are. Because of His life in us, we become more completely who we actually are, not less. Author H. Wheeler Robinson says, "In sharpest contrast with the original Buddhist solution of the mystery of life by the elimination of personality as an allusion, the Christian of all types finds an intensification and justification of his personality as the first result of His faith."[7] This is the glory of having been made in the image of God. God does not want adoring zombies, scriptural robots who have no personality and give programmable answers.

Several years ago, I attended a funeral of a beloved friend. The building was heavy with the fragrance of enormous flower arrangements (she was greatly loved by many), but the most pungent smell in the room was the perfume of a certain denomination. Everyone dressed alike, smelled alike, wore their hair alike, walked alike, and sat alike; and they had no clue how *much* alike they appeared. Do our denominations applaud conformity or diversity? Are we mentoring people in our image, or after His?

God longs to see the character and personality of Jesus expressed in the uniqueness of who we are. You have heard how little goslings are imprinted by the first thing they see. I have often wondered if that is not also true with us. Listen to someone pray for three minutes, and you will often pick up the style or tone of how someone they admired prayed. I see it particularly pronounced in young pastors who have been mentored by strong leaders. Recently I heard a young pastor say, as if it was his own thought, "I believe you do what you want, apologize later, and then turn the whole thing into a reconciliation lesson." I knew immediately who had mentored that young man. We are not mentoring people after our own personalities or preferences but pointing them to the person of Jesus, who loved them and gave Himself for them.

Professor and author Dallas Willard says it like this: "We bring the heart-wrenching goodness of God, His incomprehensible graciousness and generosity before the mind of disciples by helping them to see and understand the person of Jesus."[8] International prayer leader David Bryant tells the story of how frustrated he once felt only being a prayer leader. Surely there were other kingdom advancing things he could be doing. One night about 2:00 A.M., David felt he heard the Lord say, *Get the people to Me, and I'll take them from there.* When Jesus is the heart of our mentoring we are doing just that—getting people to Jesus. Teaching them to hear Jesus, to see Jesus in others, to find Jesus in the Word. The emphasis is more interactive than informational between Jesus and the one being mentored. Our goal is not to create clones of ourselves, but of original followers of Christ.

One of the greatest needs in this generation is for godly mentors to pour their hearts into the next generation. There are more students applying for apprenticeships in the Spirit than there are mentors available. I believe the tide will swiftly change. The Holy Spirit is highly invested in recommissioning and reactivating those who have been disappointed with spiritual authorities, those who have been disappointed with God, those who feel that God has passed them by. There are thousands of prodigals who will return to the Father's house and become mentors to the hopeless. They are going to get a new glimpse of Jesus and become mothers and fathers to the next generation. They will not put stickers on their RVs that say, "We are spending our children's inheritance." They will be fully invested in getting people to Jesus at any cost. I see a day when it will be standard practice for mothers in Israel and fathers in the faith to take new converts under their wings and introduce them to the life of Jesus.

WANTED: MOTHERS AND FATHERS IN ISRAEL

Unlike my generation, who questioned authority and did not trust anyone over thirty, one of the distinctions of this generation is they are actively seeking spiritual mothers and fathers. One youth leader overheard a young woman enthusiastically ask another, "So how many years did you have to pray to find your spiritual parents?" Then she added sadly, "I have been praying for two years and still haven't found mine."

Perhaps *you* are that girl's answer. What exactly is a mother or father in Israel? In the Old Testament the curious title "mother in Israel" occurs twice. Both times, the person herself claims the title. In Judges 5, Deborah is exalting over the victory God has just given Israel. Deborah describes herself when she says in her victory duet with Barak: "Village life ceased, it ceased in Israel, until I, Deborah, arose, arose a mother in Israel."[9] As a mother in Israel, Deborah refused to be complacent with the oppression of her people. She called men into their warrior destiny to defeat the army of Jabin. Jabin, the King of Canaan, was no mere lightweight. He had nine hundred chariots of iron and had harshly oppressed Israel for twenty years. Deborah heard from God the tactics; she heard the strategy; and she gave Barak the confidence to fulfill his role as general of the army of God. Mothers in Israel hear God. They act on what they hear. They spend their lives bringing other people into their destinies.

The second time the phrase "mother in Israel" appears is when a wise, unnamed woman questions General Joab, who is about to ransack her city. Joab is after the scoundrel Sheba, who is trying to get Israel to revolt against David as king. Joab, David's general, builds up a siege mound against the city, Abel. This brave woman calls to Joab over the wall: "They used to talk in former times, saying, 'They shall surely seek guidance at Abel,' and so they would end disputes. I am among the peaceable and faithful in Israel. You seek to destroy a city and a mother in Israel. Why would you swallow up the inheritance of the Lord?"[10] Joab quickly assures her he does not want to destroy anybody or anything but Sheba. So the woman ends up throwing fugitive want-to-be-king Sheba's head over the wall to Joab, saving her city in the process.

Mothers in Israel are concerned about the corporate whole. They are confrontational when they have to be. They want to assure the continuity of a city or person's redemptive gift. And they are wise about what needs to be done to accomplish it. Being a mother in Israel is a high and holy calling. As you grow in being one, you will find you are disinterested in your own name being known or your own welfare being protected. You will be all for your children. You will say with Deborah, "My heart is for the princes of Israel"(see Judges 5:9).

I have two "mothers in Israel" in my life. Both of them are gorgeous, and both of them happen to be named Virginia. One of them prays for my schedule regularly and calls to relay to me what she is hearing from the Lord. Virginia Smith gives me long hugs and constant encouragement. When I look at her, I see how beautiful the years look on a lover of God. She has helped me define and fine-tune my calling.

The other Virginia is a wise and powerful leader. She encourages me by showing up unexpectedly at different places where I speak. She has taught me the powerful principle of never speaking to an audience I do not love. Virginia Otis offered me this sage advice years ago, and I have never forgotten it. I used to spend most of my time in message preparation consuming a diet of Greek and Hebrew roots. Now, because of Virginia, I spend most of my time imploring Jesus to give me His heart for a particular audience. Virginia Otis's life vividly illustrates to me the tenacity and long-haul faithfulness of a lover of God. While her eyes flash brilliantly, Virginia is no flash in the pan. She has power with God because she is a lover of Jesus. Both Virginias in my life consistently point me to Him.

FATHERS IN THE FAITH

Parenting the next generation is not confined to women. Fathers in the faith are every bit as necessary as mothers in Israel. Paul was many things, an apostle, a writer, a thinker, a builder of churches. But his most significant role, I believe, was a father in the faith. There were not a whole lot of them around even in those days. Paul put the ratio of instructors in Christ to fathers at ten thousand to a few.[11] It is curious that something so necessary, so absolutely vital, is so rare. Could it be that Satan would do anything to keep men from assuming this powerful role because he knows what a horrible threat it would be to his rebellion? I believe men's finest and most enduring role is to pour their lives into the next generation. Elijah found his Elisha. We are to likewise find ours and pray for that person (or those people) a double portion of our knowledge of God.

What do spiritual fathers do? They are simply themselves. Several years ago I was in Jerusalem helping lead a conference. There were certain aspects that were difficult for me. At one point one of the speakers, Campbell McAlpine, a wise, godly man, full of the goodness of the Lord, came over and gave me a hug. It was an entirely spontaneous gesture. And it carried the weight of a freight train. I did not until that moment realize how much I longed for a father.

Fathers in the faith pour their wisdom, experiences, and lives into the next generation. They spend their lives imparting a revelation of Jesus. They do not merely teach; they inspire. They do not just lecture; they live and love truth before their children. Spiritual fathers know how to encourage.

Recently I spoke to a Presbyterian church, and at the close of the service a very well-dressed elderly man simply came over and kissed me on the cheek while I was talking with someone else. I do not know the man's name, and he had no idea what a father deficit I had. But in that simple gesture, I felt as if Jesus had kissed me.

Fathers in the faith know how to empower their children to seek Jesus. Like the gentleman who kissed me, they have a great sense of timing. They are not necessarily eloquent or highly intelligent. Paul said, "And I, brethren, when I came to you, did not come with excellence of speech or of wisdom declaring to you the testimony of God. For I determined not to know anything among you except Jesus Christ and Him crucified."[12] Jesus, and Jesus alone, is a father in the faith's sole curriculum.

You Have Wealth to Impart

I often find myself telling audiences, "Even if your whole life has been one long series of mistakes, you have wealth to impart. Sometimes knowing what *not* to do is as valuable as knowing what *to* do. Your whole life up to this point could have been simply preparation for your finest assignment. You have always had the potential for this job, but with every passing day you have become more qualified for it. Your life story is your curriculum for compassion. Your experience becomes your student's syllabus. Your heartaches can reap a plentiful harvest in another person's life. Tell your children—spiritual or physical—what Jesus has done for you. Tell them how you have found Him faithful. Tell them who you know Him to be.

Recently at a countywide Concert of Prayer, a lady named Ann Lewis went to an open microphone near the end of the service. She started singing a little children's song, "When We All Pull Together, Together." Ann has effectively ministered to and loved children for forty-five years. Love oozed from her every pore as she prayed. We had done a lot that evening—shown a powerful video on transformation of cities and had an anointed children's choir sing and pray for adults. It had been a very rich evening. But the thing that touched many people most was Ann. Ann had found Jesus faithful and precious. She had known Him to be everything He ever promised. By the time Ann was finished praying, you wanted to know this Jesus she loved.

Could mentoring really be all that simple? Just loving Jesus and letting His love touch others? I believe it is. You do not need any special credentials, any talent, or any paperwork. Do you love Jesus? Do you know Him? All you really need are two arms and two lips. Your arms are needed for embracing, and your lips for telling your personal story. How has Jesus been faithful to you? What is your story? How has your story merged with the story of Jesus? Your lips are needed to kiss the cheek of a generation desperate for touch. Your finest assignment is to tell the next generation of the greatness and gentleness of Jesus. Mentoring is all about the simplicity of loving Jesus. That is all.

Ten

Jesus, the Heart of Our Days

---

*The way we live our days, is of course,
how we live our lives.*[1]

—Annie Dillard

*The emphasis on time is a predominant feature of
prophetic thinking. The day of the Lord is more important than the House of the Lord.*[2]

—Abraham Joshua Heschel

The pastors' prayer summit had gone unusually well. There had been hours of solid scriptural praying, a marvelous gourmet lunch, and a deepening of relational possibilities. Conversations were rich. All over the room I saw people discovering each other. Everyone seemed happy to be together. I staunchly believe, as reconciliation leader John Dawson says, "God organizes His kingdom with gifts of friendship." It looked like friendships were being ignited. My eyes swept the room, and it gave me pure pleasure.

As I basked in quiet satisfaction, I was not prepared for the critique my friend gently and somewhat hesitantly gave: "Fawn, nobody thanked Jesus for what He was doing right now. Everything prayed about was in the future. I don't understand this thing that presses everyone past this moment of God's extraordinary goodness." I quickly realized it was a fair and accurate assessment.

My radar screen was scanning relationships, not prayer. I fast-forwarded all the prayers prayed. Come to think of it, everything *had* been prayed in future tense. We *had* glossed over the present goodness of God. In our craving to see the future promises of God fulfilled, we often missed the glory of Jesus in the moment.

MISSING THE GLORY OF THE MOMENT

I have been missing the glory of the moment most of my life. My friends say I was born forty; and that is pretty close to the truth. As a child I could hardly wait to grow up. I squandered my childhood, wistful for age. When I was young, Sunday school had little vision for children to be functioning members of the Body of Christ. If I was going to be useful, it was clear that I needed to age. The world was going to hell in a handbasket, and I yearned to be plucking people out of a swirl of damnation.

I grew up hearing the slogan, "I'd rather burn out for God than rust out." It was said with such gusto that it began to assume the authority of holy writ. It ingrained in me a perpetual demand to always be producing. Consequently I am always occupied. I have a very limited ability to just be. If you want to just sip tea and just watch ice melt in a glass, I am not your best companion. (I'd probably ask you to come up with some spiritual metaphor for ice melting in order to consider the time well spent.)

As a young adult I was still ravenous for the future. The rush now was for credibility. I did not know what the magic age was, but mid-forties seemed respectable. No one took you very seriously if you were in your twenties or thirties. In my heart were all these (hopefully) godly visions with no potential for realization until I aged.

TELLING TIME

Having a son later in life was a sweet and precious gift. Joel helps me to accurately tell time. As I write this Joel is ten, and the hour hand is spinning wildly. I want to unplug the clock. I want to savor his scrunched up face when he sucks on a sour Warhead candy. I want to freeze-frame the moments when he asks me impossible questions like, "Mom, did God grieve when Goliath was killed?" When the moon dances across his skin, I want to be in that moment forever. I want to chuckle with him as we watch our little family of quail, quivering with caution as they attempt to cross the street. I want to know his darling face like a fireman knows street maps. Joel has helped me realize that I must live in the *now* of Christ's goodness.

I have many deeply prophetic people in my life who are always pressing into the future. I love them and appreciate their gifts, but I have come to learn I cannot live like they do. I can not triage life because everything assumes the status of an emergency. I am tired of living a perpetually *strategic* life. (Could we permanently ban that word from Christendom?) If I don't go on extended fasts (and I very much believe in them), and pray 24/7, I have to believe God will still accomplish His purposes in the earth. I have spent a lifetime pressing into the future, and now in my mid-forties, I have no will to pursue tomorrow at the expense of today.

"Verged Out"

A friend of mine recently commented that he was "verged out." It was an interesting phrase, and it caught my ear. He explained that everyone was saying revival was just around the corner; we were on the cusp, on the verge of the greatest move of God ever. Whole nations were about to come to Jesus in a very short time. More than a billion people would turn wholeheartedly to Jesus. Stadiums would fill up because churches could not hold the harvest. Healings and miracles would be common. We needed to know what strategic times we were living in.

I have heard this on-the-cusp, on-the-verge theory for more than thirty years, and I still believe it. But I have found I cannot live in constant fervid expectancy that misses the sweetness of God in the now. This moment is all we can ever really live. This moment is sacred and holy and deserves our complete attentive focus.

Moses, the friend of God, prayed in Psalm 90:12: "So

teach us to number our days, that we may gain a heart of wisdom." How does God teach us? By helping us pay attention to our days. Moses spends the first part of Psalm 90 talking about God's agelessness, and then he contrasts it with our short life span. We are like winter's breath. We are like a blade of grass. We are an ice-cream cone, quickly scooped out and consumed. If we are to number our days, we cannot escape the brevity of our lives. Recently I spoke on this subject and had two beautiful young teenagers blow bubbles while I was speaking. That is our life span. If we do not learn to treasure this moment, what moment will we savor?

THE HOLINESS OF TIME

If we are to understand the holiness of time, we must consider that Jesus is the originator of all our days, all our moments. And we must begin at the beginning. Jesus was there when all of the worlds were created. It is easy to imagine God the Father creating everything and then introducing the Son later in history. But the New Testament is clear that God the Father made the worlds through Jesus, God the Son. In John 1:3 we see that "[a]ll things were made through Him, and without Him nothing was made that was made." And again in Hebrews 1:1-2 we read that "God, who at various times and in various ways spoke in time past to the fathers by the prophets, has in these last days spoken to us by His Son, whom He has appointed heir of all things, through whom also He made the worlds."

Our Creator will have great significance to us as we look at the holiness of time. Rabbi Abraham Joshua Heschel makes the point that in Genesis 2:3 the first thing God ever made holy in creation, was not a thing, but time.[3] "And He hallowed the seventh day." The only attachment of the word *holy* in the Ten Commandments is to the word *Sabbath*. God makes something out of nothing, hangs the universe, forms myriad creatures out of His fertile imagination. After finishing all that He takes a rest when He is not tired. By resting, He makes *time* holy. He has just made a whole universe of things, very impressive things mind you: nebulae, sea dragons, hummingbirds, humans. But His final touch, His most unexpected behavior, is rest. God makes time sacred by declaring the Sabbath day holy.

Time becomes holy in contrast to other religions that have *places or things* that are holy, such as mountains, trees, shrines, certain utensils, or sacred objects. Certainly had we been God, we would have made *things* sacred, not time. We are by nature collectors of things, and we judge each other by how many things we possess: clothes, money, furniture, properties, or other people. It is interesting to see how many *things* possess our waking moments. We spend copious time attending to their maintenance, bowing at their shrine, while the really important relationships of our lives rust with decay and neglect. Someone once said we love things and use people. That is unfortunately a pretty accurate assessment.

Heschel makes the observation that there is no equivalent for the word *thing* in biblical Hebrew. The word *davar,* which in later Hebrew came to denote "thing," means in biblical Hebrew

> 'speech: word; message; report tidings; advice, request; promise; decision; sentence; theme; story; saying; utterance; business; occupation; acts; good deeds; events; way, manner, reason; cause but never thing. Is this a sign of linguistic poverty, or rather an indication of an unwarped view of the world, of not equating reality (derived from the Latin word res, thing) with thinghood?[4]

Of course, there is nothing wrong with things when kept in proper perspective. The Word of God is clear that God gives us richly all things to enjoy (see 1 Tim. 6:17). After all, He made things. But often things begin demanding of us time that is holy. If you have a big house, it demands you take more time cleaning. If you have a big car, you have to spend more time waxing it. The more things, the more time required to maintain them. Things eat time, and time is sacred. Time has capacity for holiness.

When God made the Sabbath holy, He made a statement of our utter dependency on Him. Sabbath is an assault on our mistaken notion that our striving, our haggling (either with man or God, it makes no difference), our constant fervid expenditure of self-effort, is what we need to make our way in the world. Taking time off from the world and watching it still survive, tells us that the Lord is God, and we are not.

When God instituted the Sabbath, He was instructing us on creativity as well. Only God would create and then rest. Man's order was to rest and then create. Adam was born into sabbath. His first experience of God was a God at rest. Man was fashioned purposely so that rest was his first exposure to life. God purposed that all creativity, all produce, all effort from man would be initiated by rest. We do not rest in order to work some more. We work because we have rested. This truth has tremendous ramifications for our life with Christ.

We do not *earn* the right to rest. Rest is a gift. Rest allowed Adam to marvel at his world without having to immediately *manage* it. Rest was not intended as a reward for hard work. It was the place from which hard work initiated. Work issued from rest, not rest from work. Work is good, and labor is honorable. Paul says, "If anyone will not work, neither shall he eat." [5] Work is necessary, but life is not primarily about work. Dr. Tony Campolo recently told a graduating class at Gordon College:

> Today we're told by culture that we need to work, work, work. We lose track of who we are—why we're here to begin with . . . don't simply be a replacement part for someone else who can do the same job . . . we need to take time to pray more . . . sit still and wait for God to invade us, to transform our minds, to change us. If you have no time to be still, there will be no ecstasy in your life. [6]

Being friends with Jesus is about rest and trust; not about pushing, pulling, stressing, and striving. We can try with all our might to accomplish character change either in ourselves or in society, and find our efforts lead to little lasting change. Life does not flow out of our own efforts, no matter how virtuous that effort may be. Life flows out of Jesus, the Prince of Life. He is our complete source. In Him, we have been *given* all things that pertain to life and godliness (see 2 Peter 1:3).

Jesus said "Take my yoke upon you and learn from Me, for I am gentle and lowly in heart, and you will find rest for your souls."[7] I read that verse and think, *I need to put on His yoke, slog through the harvest, put in a good sixteen-hour day, memorize the facts about His character, and then, then at last, I will find rest for my soul.* No, no, no. Jesus' yoke is that you rest when He rests; you work when He works; you match your movements with the rhythms of His grace. Jesus moved this way with the Father. He said, "The Son can do nothing by himself, he can only do what he sees the Father do."[8] If we diligently push ahead by ourselves, we end up with a chafed neck and serious yoke burn.

THE PRIORITY OF RELATIONSHIP

When God made time holy, He established for us the priority of relationship over every other thing. The Sabbath is meant to be spent relating to God and to each other. Adam's eyelids fluttered open to a world of wonder. The breath God breathed in him was no doubt hurriedly spent in a stream of questions. The Sabbath was a day for observing, a day for cherishing, a day to saturate one's soul in the pleasantness of God.

Sabbath for us is time to remember God's goodness, His provision. It creates for us an interior photo album of God's tenderness in our life. We were to remember His work not only in creation, but in the collected stories of God's intervention in our history. The very act of remembering is a community event.

You could, I suppose, go off by yourself and recount God's goodness like some sort of monastic Lone Ranger. But in the history of the Jews, the recounting was always relational. God stories were to be told in the family, around the fire, in the assembly. God stories were the three-dimensional glasses that helped you understand your own unique personal history. There was no way to understand your story without understanding the collective story. Our whole life story is but a sentence in the grand story, His story. Our individual sentences were never meant to make sense all by themselves.

In my freshman year in college, I read for a blind friend. On top of my own required reading, I read for many of her classes as well. Occasionally I'd think how much nicer my transcript might look if I spent all my energy on my own classes. But God was teaching me the priority of relationship and interconnectedness. My grades meant nothing to God if to get them I ignored what He valued. God prizes the relational aspects of our lives far more than He ever values academic success. If you ignore people, you might get an "A" on a transcript and get an "unsatisfactory" from God.

Life is all about relationship. And building relationship with God and each other takes time. The success of our lives in the end is measured by how well we loved, not how well we produced. When people stand around our grave they are not going to count how many books we wrote, sermons we preached, or companies we founded. They are going to recount that they felt loved by us, that we gave them hope. That we called out of them giftings and abilities they did not know they had. When God made time holy on the seventh day, He highlighted the fact that man's spiritual and relational development had priority over the brawny, hurly-burly mandate of subduing and occupying the earth.

JESUS, OUR SABBATH

Could it be that the pronounced emphasis on observing the Sabbath throughout the Old Testament was, again, one more arrow pointing us to Jesus? Not once every seven days, but moment by moment, second by second, Jesus is our rest. He can be savored and enjoyed. We can cease striving and know He is God. We can cease trying to be perfect, and know that He is our righteousness; He is our peace; He is everything that could ever be required of us. With Jesus we never need to postpone our peace, and there is no need to postpone our enjoyment. We do not ever have to live under the heavy sentence, "Not now; wait until I finish my work." We never need to postpone our joy. That comes as good news if you are anything like I am, a worker droid who never rests easily. When Jesus uttered "It is finished," it was. It's all done, and we cannot add a thing to it. Our perpetual Sabbath began the moment Jesus gave Himself on the cross.

Because Jesus is our continual sabbath, He sanctifies our work. There is now no contradiction between Sabbath and work, because one flows out of the other very naturally. Jesus is our sabbath, and He is the one working within us, both willing and doing His good pleasure. Every moment of ordinariness can become holy because we live in Him, and He is holy. There is no division between the sacred and the secular.

NO SECULAR/SACRED DIVIDE

Tom Howard in his beautiful little book *The Splendor of the Ordinary* says,

> The secularization of life urged on us by science and commerce and modernity generally is surely one of the bleakest myths ever to settle down over men's imagination . . . we have to recover the sense of the hallowed as being all around us. We will have to open our eyes and try to see once more the commonplace as both cloaking and revealing the holy to us.[9]

Fixing oatmeal or fixing a tire can be just as sacramental as bowing to pray. When people asked with incredulity,

> "'Lord, when did We see you hungry and feed You, or thirsty and give You drink? When did we see You a

stranger and take You in, or naked and clothe You? Or when did we see You sick, or in prison and come to You?' And the King will answer and say to them, 'Assuredly, I say to you, inasmuch as you did it to one of the least of these My brethren, you did it to Me.'"[10]

Sometimes "the least of these," is someone in our own family looking up to us with hungry eyes. It is holy work to feed them. Jewish philosopher Abraham Joshua Heschel says, "Something sacred is at stake in every event."[11] Because Jesus is our continual Sabbath, there is no division between the sacred and the secular. Jesus is Lord of both. His holiness pervades the mundane as well as the heavenly. All times are holy because He is Lord of time.

THE LORD OF POTS AND PANS

Brother Lawrence was one man who knew the sacrament of the moment. He jokingly called himself the "Lord of Pots and Pans." A seventeenth-century Parisian Carmelite monk, he understood the integrity of common life, the hallowedness of the ordinary. For him, the presence of Jesus was just as real while he was scouring a pot as when he was in chapel saying Mass. He was a humble monastery cook who simply kept himself in the love of God. He practiced the presence of God by keeping himself in continual conversation with God.

In 1692, his book *The Practice of the Presence of God* was written as a compilation of letters. That little book has nourished millions of readers for three hundred years. Brother Lawrence thoroughly enjoyed the presence of Jesus in the present moment. It did not matter if he was buying wine for the monastery, dicing up vegetables, or boiling potatoes. The ordinariness of the activity did not matter. He had resolved in his heart to do everything not to please man but for the love of God. Jesus was constantly present to Him. Cardinals, theologians, and even the Pope came to see him to learn his secret.

How did Brother Lawrence learn to so enjoy Jesus in the moment? How did he come to find the simplicity of devotion to Christ so rich, so satisfying? We might think that the ability to enjoy Jesus moment by moment in the ordinariness of life to be quite beyond us (especially if you are the mother of preschoolers). We often forget that many saints had wives or servants that made it easier to concentrate on the eternal. But Brother Lawrence had no wife, and he *was* the servant. Was life less demanding in those days? Were there fewer distractions in a quiet monastery? Perhaps Brother Lawrence was born with saint tendencies.

But Brother Lawrence was no stranger to human appetites. He was quick to repent of his sins and leave them with God. He found mortification useless. He was by his own description, "a great awkward fellow who broke everything." He went into the monastery hoping to smart for his awkwardness. He wanted to sacrifice his life to God and renounce pleasure, but God sorely disappointed him. He had found instead, much to his surprise, nothing but satisfaction. For fifteen years he worked in a kitchen, a place he never would have chosen. In that kitchen he found no sacred/secular divide. "The time of business," said he, "does not with me differ from the time of prayer; and in the noise and clutter of my kitchen, while several persons are at the same time calling for different things, I possess God in as great tranquillity as if I were upon my knees at the Blessed Supper."[12] Brother Lawrence, by nourishing high thoughts of God and speaking continually to Him about all matters, no matter how small, found his soul at a perpetual feast. He knew by experience that all times are holy.

JESUS SAVES ME NOW

Hannah Whitall Smith, a wise Quaker woman who wrote *The Christian's Secret To A Happy Life* more than one hundred years ago, said: "Settle down on this one thing, Jesus came to save you *now*, in this life, from the power and dominion of sin, and to make you more than a conqueror through His power." She continues, "Perhaps no four words have more meaning in them than the following, which I would have you repeat over and over with your voice and with your soul,

> *Jesus* saves me now. It is He.
> Jesus *saves* me now. It is His work to save.
> Jesus saves *me* now. I am the one to be saved.
> Jesus saves me *now*. He is doing it every moment."[13]

Jesus is the heart of our days because He is the heart of our moments. I remember a sweet, godly woman embracing me once when I was young. She said, "Sweetheart, you've heard the song, 'Day by Day'?" I had. She shook her head and continued, "I have found I cannot live like that with Jesus. A day is much too long. I have to live with Him moment by moment." I am learning the truth of her words. A day is much too long. I cannot keep Jesus in my thoughts for a whole day. But I can for just this moment and the next. As a child there was an old hymn we used to sing that I loved and still find sweet.

> Moment by moment, I am kept in His love,
> Moment by moment, I have life from above.
> Looking to Jesus, till glory doth shine,
> Moment by moment, Oh Lord I am thine.[14]

We are His, completely and utterly His. All we have to do at this moment is look to Him, the keeper of our days, the author and finisher of our story.

Eleven

Jesus, the Heart
of Our Future

---

*Christianity must stand or fall by the finality
of Christ as to life and it's destiny."* [1]

—P. T. FORSYTHE

Afraid she might insult or offend God, the young girl paused and then asked softly, "Mom, is worship *all* we are going to do in heaven?" The mother replied that God indeed had much more in mind. We hadn't endured all the challenges of earth to just sit cross-legged before the throne singing "Kum Ba Yah" year after year. Oh no! We were intended to share Christ's throne, to rule and reign forever with Him, world without end. Heaven was going to be beyond our wildest dreams. It would be full on, high-impact adventure that would make your hair stand on end. Adventure that would make Indiana Jones seem like a bona fide sissy. The girl listened skeptically, not convinced. The desirability of heaven still seemed an open question.

I can relate to my young friend's concern. My introduction to heaven was in pea-soup-colored Sunday school rooms, fiddling with (and sometimes when no one was looking, eating) dried out play dough, and watching flimsy flannel graph pictures. It was all pitiful, colorless, and stale. Heaven sounded dull and terribly unappealing. All the hymns and popular songs described it as the ultimate retirement home. I was not sure I would last through eons of boredom, but the other alternative did not sound all that appealing either. What was I to do? My choices were either bland or terrifying.

OUR ROLE IN SCRIPTURE

To understand what awaits us, we need to clear the deck of our preconceptions and begin with the One who knows all things. Our future is spelled out clearly in Scripture. God's holy ambitions for us are astonishing—the last thing we would expect. We flinch at the audacity of God to even consider it. Our destiny, according to Scripture, is one of reigning and ruling with Christ. We are not going to float around on ether passively thrumming out-of-tune harps. Oh, no! God has much more in mind. Revelation 22:5 tells us, "There shall be no night there: They need no lamp nor light of the sun, for the Lord God gives them light. And they shall reign forever and ever."[2] Paul tells Timothy, "If we endure, we shall also reign with Him."[3] On the isle of Patmos, the apostle John overhears the four living creatures and the twenty-four elders singing this new song about Jesus: "You are worthy to take the scroll, and to open its seals; for You were slain, and have redeemed us to

God by Your blood out of every tribe and tongue and people and nation, and have made us kings and priests to our God; and we shall reign on the earth."[4] Then, just in case we are thinking that all this ruling and reigning stuff is way off into the future, Paul contrasts Adam's sin with Jesus' obedience and says, "For if by the one man's offense death reigned through the one, much more those who receive abundance of grace and of the gift of righteousness will reign in life through the One, Jesus Christ."[5] The Scripture is quite clear. We were designed to rule and reign with Christ.

CHILDREN'S STORIES FREIGHTED WITH CLUES

Nobel Prize winner Elie Wiesel said, "God made man because He loves stories."[6] We love them too. Perhaps the reason we love them is because they are so full of things we intuitively know, yearnings we have in the depths of us that we have never found words for and have barely even hoped to expect, long-lost memories of a destiny that awaits us, beyond telling.

Stories often come the closest to awakening eternity in our hearts. Children's stories come freighted with clues to our future. Stories arouse our hearts in a deeply-felt way. When we hear stories of how someone overcame all odds, all obstacles, and ended up a king or queen, we find those particular stories resonant beyond explanation. Stories have universal appeal. As any parent can tell you, the four most common words of young children besides, "What can I eat?" are, "Tell me a story." This power of story explains the potent appeal of books such as *The Chronicles of Narnia* series, by C. S. Lewis. Lewis masterfully presents a vivid, engaging picture of our present and future ruling and reigning with Christ. Narnia is real and real people go there. The thrones at Cair Paravel are still waiting to be filled. You know they belong to you.

PREPARATION AND EDUCATION

This life is merely preparation and education for the real thing. Earth is God's Graduate School of Apprenticeship. This is where we learn compassion, patience, wisdom, and self-control. If we are not going to need these qualities of soul later, why does God spend so much time teaching them to us now? The fruit of the Spirit is not a collection of character qualities to correct our fallen nature. The fruit of the Spirit is the personality of Jesus. If the Holy Spirit is imparting His character to us, there must be an eventual place for its expression beyond just this life. Why would we need compassion in heaven? Of what use would there be for self-control? If heaven is merely a place of eternal comfort for the miseries of life here on earth, most of what the Holy Spirit is teaching us now is irrelevant.

Our life here on earth is just a microfraction of the real thing. This life is rigorous preparation for a ruling and reign-ing life, world without end. In light of this fact, we can see the pain of today differently. Where our difficult circumstances on earth seem meaningless, they begin to take on purpose as we consider them as an apprenticeship for the throne.

A Senseless Universe

We must be honest about it. Life appears senseless. There are promises from God that go unfulfilled. Earth's history bleeds with the tale of barbarous wars, brutal domestic violence, victims who might easily say like Job, "Cursed is the womb that gave me birth." There are women routinely mutilated through female circumcision. Slaves are still traded, and children are horribly exploited.

We in the West spend billions on diet plans, while thousands of children die every day from malnutrition and hunger. This life is not just or kind or fair. And if this life is all there is, we have ample reason for despair. The story line does not make sense. If this is all there is, the existentialists are right. Jean Paul Sartre's purposeless universe and hopelessness are all we can expect. From a Christian perspective, if heaven is mainly just a consummate retirement community where we will be eternally comforted, all the pain and heartache of earth is pointless. Much more than we need comfort, we need meaning. There must be an emotionally satisfying reason for the excruciating ache of history.

Our Future Shrouded in Mysteries

Our future is shrouded in holy, immense mystery. Try as we might, we cannot lift the weighty veil. We see dimly through smudged glasses. This fact has plagued philosophers for centuries. How can you find a story line in merely the preface? If you are looking at your misery purely in the context of this life, it *is* fearfully and pitifully terrible. If this is the main event, Solomon was right when he said, "The race is not to the swift, nor the battle to the strong, nor bread to the wise, nor riches to men of understanding, nor favor to men of skill; but time and chance happen to them all."[7] Solomon observed life from a restricted vantage point. His observations were similar to a frog in the bottom of a well, making observations on the circle of light at the top. When we see life from God's view though, an entirely different picture emerges.

YOUR PAIN IS NOT IN VAIN

Because life is an apprenticeship, your pain is not in vain. In some unknown way your exact circumstance is preparing you for something very specific. Perhaps you have wept at the grave of your child. Your mind has reeled at the senselessness of it all. People prayed, they fasted; they told you God would heal her. Now God appears untrustworthy. All the platitudes and frail words of man are just so much noise. Mental and spiritual equilibrium is, for you, an ancient memory. God is far from your groaning, and yet you have nowhere else to turn.

Your story does not end at your death or at the death of your loved one. C. S. Lewis says it well: "For us, it's the end of the story . . . but for them it was only the beginning of the real story. All their life . . . had been the cover and title page: now at last they were beginning Chapter One of the great Story, which no one on earth has read: which goes on forever: in which every chapter is better than the one before."[8] Because of His sacrifice, your story and future, loved one, is indivisible from His.

Maybe, as a child, the greedy hand of lust snatched for itself a part of you it never owned. You have blamed yourself, thinking somehow you deserved it. You have been violated, and you find yourself crushed and bruised and desperate for genuine love. Or perhaps you are, right now, being slandered and divorced against your will. You thought this spouse was God's choice. People seemed to agree; yes indeed, this was the one. You have tried counseling. You have prayed. And now this person is trying to steal your inheritance. They are assaulting the core of who you are, shedding blood with their tongue, and wreaking havoc on your reputation.

You may be swimming through a bay of question marks, the undercurrent pulling you farther and farther away from the shore of certainty. You question God's faithfulness. You may have spent a lifetime with all your theological ducks in a row and find now they have flown off in different directions. Things you would have been willing to die for only a decade ago now barely rouse your heart.

Whatever has pierced your soul and bled your hope for the future, wherever evil has had its sway, your story does not end with your life here on earth. Even if tragedy has been your companion from birth, there is glorious redemption in your future. This life is not, nor ever has been, all there is.

Jesus' suffering proves to us that our pain is not in vain. For lovers of Jesus, Isaiah's prophecy is almost too holy and terrible to read.

> He is despised and rejected by men, a Man of sorrows and acquainted with grief, and we hid, as it were, our faces from Him; He was despised, and we did not esteem Him. Surely He has borne our griefs and carried our sorrows; yet we esteemed Him stricken, smitten by God and afflicted. But He was wounded for our transgressions, He was bruised for our iniquities; the chastisement for our peace was upon Him, and by His stripes we are healed.⁹

And what did all that bruising of the priceless Son of God achieve?

If you look on the surface, Jesus' pain looks in vain. At the culmination of His life on earth, when He was received up into heaven, there were perhaps only 500 people gathered to watch. You can get 500 people pretty easily to a soccer match. And forty days later there were only 120 people left in the upper room. Certainly not much to show for God's crowning moment in history. God empties His treasury in giving us Jesus and, only weeks after He is gone, there are just a pitiful few still following. If we just looked at Jesus' life in the natural, it would seem an abject failure.

But Jesus' life on this earth was not the end of His story. Millions of people all over the earth have come to cherish and serve Him. A long procession from every tribe and tongue at all points of history have willingly given their lives to and for Him. Strong men unashamedly weep out loud for love of Him. Women serve Him in hostile lands, pouring out the alabaster box of their devotion at His feet. Children, often His most ardent lovers, close their eyes at night and seek His care. He shakes kingdoms, deconstructs ancient thrones, and causes empires to crumble. He melts hardened hearts with just a glance. Jesus craters into the hopelessness of our story and forever alters its orbit and changes its ending.

His kingdom is relentlessly advancing all over the earth. If we judge the fruit of Jesus' suffering from the standpoint of His thirty-three years, we miss the point. His suffering enormously impacts all future history. Christ indeed, "lifted with His pierced hands empires off their hinges and turned the stream of centuries out of its channel."[10]

Jesus proves to us we cannot ever fully judge this moment by this moment. We only see clearly through eternity's eyes. Our future is not limited to tomorrow. Our destiny and the promises of God are not limited to our life on earth. This life is simply preliminary to our real story. God has a plan for us that eye has not seen nor ear heard. Our today is preparation for an astonishing role tomorrow. Timothy says, "Finally, there is laid up for me, the crown of righteousness, which the Lord, the righteous judge, will give to me on that Day, and not to me only but also to all who love his appearing."[11] Jesus has crowns, and He is passing them out. They are not Cracker Jack crowns. They are real diadems, signifying real rulership. Responding aright to this moment qualifies you to receive it.

This life is an apprenticeship for ruling and reigning with Christ. We do not know how our own individual circumstance on this earth prepares us exactly. We cannot figure it out based on observation. Some of us grew up in wonderful homes; others of us were berated, verbally or physically abused. Some of us have married faithful and tender spouses, and others have not. But each of us, no matter how good or bad our lives may be, has our own private heartache, our own secret places of despair. Each of us can use this moment to qualify for an inheritance of rulership.

It is our response to this life that prepares us for ruling and reigning with Christ. Prayer particularly prepares us. In prayer, we learn to hear God's voice; we start thinking about situations as He thinks about them. In prayer our hearts are enlarged, and we start caring about people in other countries, countries whose names we may not even be able to pronounce. In prayer we see the larger scope of the kingdom. Prayer expands the borders of our being. It moves us beyond only caring for our own little limited circle of concern. Prayer is God's unsurpassed training course for the throne. When we learn to pray Scripture we find our heart desiring His fame, His renown, to cover the earth. We long for people to love and obey Him in fresh new ways. We want to see every person on earth find their joy in Him.

OBEDIENCE IS NOT AN OPTION

Obedience prepares us as well. Have you ever wondered how you could show your love for Jesus in greater ways?

Be swift to obey. Obedience is not an option for a genuine disciple. Instant obedience is the fastest way to prove the faithfulness of God. My husband owes his life to an act of instant obedience. He was in Thailand, directing a forklift operator picking up a pile of wood. As the forklift carried its load, coiled underneath was a deadly snake ready to strike Joey. The forklift operator could not see the snake, but fortunately he saw Joey's hand movement directing him to dump the load. Even though it did not make sense, he instantly obeyed, dropped the load, and killed the six-foot cobra. Our instant obedience will often preserve life.

What would the world look like if, tomorrow morning, those of us who loved God began to instantly obey every prompting of the Holy Spirit? What would change? I challenge you, dear reader, to start obeying. When you read the Word, ask yourself, "Am I doing this?" If not, ask Jesus to show you how to begin.

If this life was the main event, the real story, and heaven was just the afterward, why do you suppose obedience occupies such a prominent place in Scripture? We do not qualify for heaven based on our own efforts. Doing everything right will not buy us one hour of salvation. Jesus' blood is our entire redemption. We can add nothing to His sacrifice. So why is obedience important if it does not buy our entrance into heaven? Because obedience has far-reaching consequences beyond just our earthly life. Could it be that learning to obey the slight nudging of the Holy Spirit now will affect how we rule and reign later?

JESUS, NOT JUST FUTURE BUT PRESENT

Of course, I do not mean to say that everything is just for your tomorrows. Jesus saves us now. He is available to save you this very moment. He is the I am; not the "I was," or "I will be." David said in Psalm 27:13, "I would have lost heart, unless I had believed that I would see the goodness of the Lord In the *land of the living.*" Do not postpone your joy. God's mercies are new every morning and great is His faithfulness. Jesus is just as present now as He ever will be then, if we have the eyes of faith to see it. We are a people with a strong unmovable ancient/future/now hope. Because we are in Christ, His present is our present; His destiny is our destiny; His future is our future. We do not have to slog through our sorrows and just hang on till heaven. He is as fully ours now as He will ever be then. "God is our refuge and strength, A very present help in trouble."[12]

But His presence does not always change our present circumstance. His presence does not make us immune to the fact that people we love die. Debilitating illnesses stalk our parents. Sometimes our children make foolish choices. Relationships shatter. Promises made in the fires of love fail in the light of reality. Jesus said, "In the world you will have tribulation."[13] And we have sadly found that to be all too true.

Jesus gives us meaning, as we understand His far-ranging intent for our lives, an intent that Paul prays in Ephesians 1:18: "I pray that your heart will be flooded with light so that you can see something of the future He has called you to share"(TLB). Heaven is Jesus. He is the fountain of all being, life, goodness. Our future is dense with a muscular intergalactic destiny forever tied to His—a *real life adventure* that makes *Star Wars* appear pallid and primitive. We were not created to simply be adoring zombies. All our days on earth were simply preparation for the real thing. We will be as His bride, coregents with Christ. John talks about our future like this: "Beloved, now we are children of God; and it has not yet been revealed what we shall be, but we know that when He is revealed, we shall be like Him, for we shall see Him as He is."[14]

Our earthly life is merely the title page and opening chapter. C. S. Lewis talked of a day when "we will remember the galaxies as an old tale." The entire purpose of history is to prepare for Jesus, the Lamb of God, a Bride made up of every tribe and tongue, who will rule and reign with Him world without end.[15] Jesus said, "To him who overcomes I will grant to sit with Me on My throne, as I also overcame and sat down with My Father on His throne."[16] All of history is to prepare a bride for the Lamb. If that bride will rule and reign with Christ, it presupposes there is something to reign over. God is not making up stuff, tricking us with some kind of exaggerated metaphor. We will actually reign with Jesus as coregents, coheirs. We are destined to share His throne. Paul says almost incredulously "Do you not know that the saints will judge the world? . . . Do you not know we shall judge angels?"[17]

Author Paul E. Billheimer says:

This royalty and rulership is no hallow, empty, figurative, symbolical, or emblematic thing. It is not a figment of the imagination. The church, the Bride, the eternal companion is to sit with Him on His throne. If His throne represents reality, then hers is no fantasy . . . all that precedes the marriage supper of the Lamb is preliminary and preparatory. Only thereafter will God's program for the eternal ages begin to unfold.[18]

LOVING HIS APPEARING IN THE PRESENT AND THE FUTURE

When Paul talks about loving His appearing, he was obviously talking about Jesus' future return to earth. But loving His appearing is not confined to some end-time scenario, some eschatological hope, when Jesus splits the skies. Jesus is present in this very moment for those who love His appearing. He appears when we welcome Him. He appears when we make room for Him. He appears when we least expect it, like He did to the disciples when He walked through the wall. He appears *in* people we least expect, like when the Holy Spirit fell on the Gentiles and confounded what up to that point had been clear, clean orthodoxy. He appears *to* people we would never dream, like Saul of Tarsus on the Damascus Road. He appears where we least expect, such as on the beach fixing breakfast for His disciples when they had given up on fishing for men and decided to go back to the more practical job of fishing for fish. He appears in our *now*, in this present moment to love and heal and bring joy to our lives. Jesus is Lord of Time, our time. This moment is just as subject to His Lordship as eternity will be when we rule and reign with Him. Those who love Him are looking for Him everywhere, all ways.

If we have eyes for Him, Jesus is not like Waldo, lost somewhere in the crowd. He is brilliantly present everywhere we look, filling our vision with wonder and awe. Elizabeth saw Him when pregnant Mary came to visit. Because Elizabeth loved His appearing, Jesus was recognizable to her even in embryonic form. Simeon recognized Jesus when he was still a pink-faced eight-day-old. When everyone else saw just another baby, Anna saw Christ. When the disciples saw just another beachcomber, John recognized Jesus, and Peter jumped out of the boat half-naked. Do we love His appearing? Do we see Him when He comes to us in prison garb, in gardener's overhauls, in the sticky hands of a smiling five-year-old? Are we learning to discern His many disguises?

The Spirit and the Bride say, "Come!"

When we think of Christ as our future, we need to be aware, as renewal scholar Donald Mostrom writes,

> of how Christ is moving in the midst of his Church toward the end of all things, and equally aware of our deep and immediate intimacy with him. The one who dwells in the midst of his Church is bringing closure to our present age.

We cannot help but have a strong sense of living at the edge of the final consummation . . . and we cannot live close to him without a strong sense of what is surely coming and how near it is. We breathe the very air of the impending Kingdom![19]

And so we join with the Spirit of God, and say "Come, Lord Jesus! To your seeking Church, come. In fresh manifestations of your glory, come. With hope for our times, come. In genuine world revival, come. For the sake of my own nation, come. Among all the nations, come. And finally—hallelujah!—In the consummation itself, come. Come. Come."[20] Even so, come Lord Jesus.

Afterword

We began this book observing how Jesus many times is not the heart of our story. Good things easily distract us from Him—even the very things meant to draw us toward Him. We have looked at practical ways to grant Him the preeminence He deserves in our thinking and practice. We have explored ways to make Jesus the heart of our story in our relationships and our message to other cultures. We are learning to look for Him, to love His appearing, to say with the Holy Spirit of God, "Come, Lord Jesus!" Come this very moment into my everyday existence. Come into my friendships. Be my great and constant joy. We know our future is inseparably linked with His. The destiny of Jesus is our destiny. To have Him is to have it all.

As a child I heard a story that perfectly wraps up this book. The details have changed through the years, but the essentials are the same. The story goes like this:

A wealthy man and his son loved to collect rare works of art. They had everything in their collection, from Picasso to Raphael. They would often sit together and admire the great works of art. When the Vietnam conflict broke out, the son went to war. He was very courageous and died in battle while rescuing another soldier. The father was notified and grieved deeply for his son.

Several months later, just before Christmas, there was a knock at the door. A young man stood at the door with a large package in his hands. He said, "Sir, you do not know me, but I am the soldier for whom your son gave his life. He saved many lives that day and he was carrying me to safety when a bullet struck him in the heart and he died instantly. He often talked about you and your love of art." The young man held out his package. "I know this isn't much. I am not really a great artist, but I think your son would have wanted you to have this." The father opened the package. It was a portrait of his son, painted by the young man. He stared in awe at the way the soldier had captured the personality of his son in the painting. The father was so drawn to the eyes that his own eyes welled up with tears. He thanked the young man and offered to pay him for the picture. "Oh, no sir, I could never repay what your son did for me. It's a gift."

The father hung the portrait over his mantel. Every time visitors came to his home he took them to see the portrait of his son before he showed them any of the other great works he had collected. The man died a few months later. There was to be a great auction of his paintings. Many influential people gathered, excited over seeing the great paintings and having an opportunity to purchase one for their collection. On the platform sat the painting of his son. The auctioneer pounded his gavel.

"We will start the bidding with the picture of the son. Who will bid for this picture?" There was silence. Then a voice in the back of the room shouted, "We want to see the famous paintings. Skip this one." But the auctioneer persisted. "Will someone bid for this painting? Who will start the bidding? $100, $200?" Another voice shouted angrily. "We did not come to see this painting. We came to see the Van Goghs, the Rembrandts. Get on with the real bids!" But still the auctioneer continued. "The son! The son! Who'll take the son?"

Finally a voice came from the very back of the room. It was the longtime gardener of the man and his son. "I'll give $10 for the painting." Being a poor man, it was all he could afford.

"We have $10, who will bid $20?" "Give it to him for $10. Let's see the masters." "$10 is the bid, will not someone bid $20?" The crowd was becoming angry. They did not want the picture of the son. They wanted the more worthy investments for their collections. The auctioneer pounded the gavel. "Going once, twice, sold for $10!"

A man sitting on the second row shouted. "Now let's get on with the collection!" The auctioneer laid down his gavel. "I am sorry, the auction is over."

"What about the paintings?"

"I am sorry. When I was called to conduct this auction, I was told of a secret stipulation in the will. I was not allowed to reveal that stipulation until this time. Only the painting of the son would be auctioned. Whoever bought that painting would inherit the entire estate, including the paintings. The man who gets the son gets everything!"

When we have Jesus, we indeed have everything. Adrian Rogers says it succinctly; "When you have said Jesus, you have said it *all*."[1]

Appendix

A Statement of Repentance to This Generation

A good man leaves an inheritance to his children's children,
but the wealth of the sinner is stored up for the righteous.

—PROVERBS 13:22

Believing God's high and holy ambition for you includes being cherished by loving, attentive, godly parents, we confess our generation's grievous sin toward you of self-centeredness, self-absorption, and self-preoccupation. Worshiping at the altar of our own fulfillment, we prized our pleasure, putting our standard of living and careers above your right to live and be nourished with tender, emotionally-present parents.

After sacrificing forty million of you on the altar of convenience, those of you who survived experienced our abdication from our God-assigned role in your life. We laid you at the feet of daycare, schools, baby-sitters, and entertainment. We did not accept the sacred privilege of mentoring you and calling you into your high and holy destiny of loving and knowing God.

Because Jesus was not the heart of our story, we did not impart to you a knowledge of the Holy One. We failed to point you to Him. We did not nurture you in the ways of God. You did not see in us the fruit of a godly, disciplined life. For those of you raised in church, we confess our lack of vision in training you to use your natural and spiritual gifts in meaningful ways. We did not take you seriously. We put in videos when we should have been pouring out our hearts.

Because all sin is a sin against relationship, we have sinned against you in not modeling loyalty in our marriages and commitments. We have failed to demonstrate to you through our relationships the unconditional love and loyalty of God. God desired that you would know Him through how we loved and cherished you. We repent of our abject failure in showing you God's character and personality. We desire the fruit of our repentance to be proved by using our influence to promote you, our resources to support you, our prayers to empower and bless you, our arms to embrace and hold you.

May you experience the complete acceptance of the Father. May Jesus heal the wounds you have sustained through our indifference and immaturity. May you be nurtured by many fathers and mothers who know the heart of God for you. May you forgive us, and become the generation that seeks Him. Though we have failed you, we commend you to the One who can redeem all things, to the One who is faithful and true, to the One who is passionately committed to you. We entrust you to the One who will never fail nor forsake you, to the One who alone can makes all things new.

Notes

PREFACE

1. For the full funeral address by Rev. Dan Beeby regarding Lesslie Newbigin, contact http://www.ship-of-fools.com/Archive/Features98 Newbigin/NewbiginBeeby.html

2. *The Confessions of St. Augustine,* translated by Rex Warner (New York: New American Library/ Mentor, 1963), 27, 235.

CHAPTER ONE

1. William Hendriksen, as quoted in John Blanchard's *Gathered Gold* (Durham, England: Evangelical Press, 1984), 171-173.

2. I would like to express my appreciation to David Bryant for suggesting the story of Augustin Jean Fresnel as we discussed the formation of this book. For more information about Augustin Jean

Fresnel's accomplishments, you will find an interesting article in the August 1999 issue of the *Smithsonian* magazine, *Science Makes a Better Lighthouse Lens*, by Bruce Watson.

3. Charles Colson, *How Now Shall We Live* (Wheaton, IL: Tyndale, 1999), 303.

4. C.S. Lewis, *An Anthology of George MacDonald* (London: Geoffrey Bles, 1945).

5. A. W. Tozer, *The Knowledge of the Holy* (Fort Washington, PA: Christian Literature Crusade).

6. John 12:21

7. Kathleen Norris, *Amazing Grace: A Vocabulary of Faith* (New York: Riverhead Books, 1996), 23.

8. P.T. Forsythe, *The Person and Place of Jesus Christ* (London: Independent Press, 1909), 242.

9. David Bryant, *The Hope At Hand* (Grand Rapids, MI: Baker, 1996), 74.

10. Roy and Revel Hession, *We Would See Jesus,* (Fort Washington, PA: Christian Literature Crusade, 1958), 48.

11. Bryant, *The Hope At Hand*.

CHAPTER TWO

1. Walter Kaiser, *Toward an Old Testament Theology* (Grand Rapids, MI: Zondervan, 1978), 42.

2. John 5:46

3. John 14:9

4. See 2 Corinthians 5:19.

5. Hession, *We Would See Jesus,* 23.

6. Matthew 4:4

7. Psalm 119:11

8. Joshua 1:8

9. John 15:7

10. John 5:39

11. Michael Horton, as quoted in the Introduction to the *Jesus Discovery Bible* (Grand Rapids, MI: Zondervan, 1999).

12. As quoted in Leonard Sweet, *SoulTsunami* (Grand Rapids, MI: Zondervan, 1999), 197.

13. E. Stanley Jones, *The Christ of the Every Road* (New York: The Abingdon Press, 1930).

14. Veronica Black, *A Vow of Silence* (New York: Ivy Books, 1992).

15. Hession, *We Would See Jesus,*16.

16. Thomas Merton, *The Silent Life* (New York: Giroux 1978), 14–15.

17. Earl D. Radmacher, general editor, *The Nelson Study Bible, New King James Version* (Nashville: Thomas Nelson, 1997) 911.

18. John R. W. Stott, *Basic Christianity* (Downers Grove, IL: InterVarsity, 1958), 23–25.

19. Richard Foster, *Prayer: Finding The Heart's True Home* (San Francisco: HarperSanFrancisco, 1992), 146.

20. A. J. Dawson, *Women of Destiny Bible* (Nashville: Thomas Nelson, 2000), Preface.

21. Revelation 1:11

22. Hosea 14:8

23. John 16:14

CHAPTER THREE

1. Kathleen Norris, *Cloister Walk* (New York: Riverhead Books, 1996), 155.

2. C. S. Lewis, *Letters to Malcolm: Chiefly on Prayer* (New York: Harcourt, Brace and World, 1964), 90.

3. Eugene Peterson, *Answering God* (San Francisco: HarperCollins, 1989), 75.

4. Foster, *Prayer: Finding the Heart's True Home* Preface.

5. Matthew 23:13

6. John 6:37

7. Colossians 1:16, 17, 18b

8. Eugene Peterson, *The Message* (Colorado Springs, CO: NavPress, 1993), Revelation 1:18.

9. Exodus 34:6,7

10. As quoted in Hession, *We Would See Jesus,* 20.

11. Colossians 1:19

12. John Piper, *A Hunger for God: Desiring God Through Fasting and Prayer* (Crossway Books, 1997).

13. Isaiah 29:13

14. Psalm 43:2

15. John 14:15

16. Story related by Pastor Mike Pilavachi in *Soul Survivor Magazine*, England, copyright 1999, used by permission.

17. Matt Redman © 1997 Kingsway's Thankyou Music, administered by EMI Publishing.

CHAPTER FOUR

1. Dallas Willard, *The Divine Conspiracy* (San Francisco: HarperCollins, 1998), 296.

2. 1 Peter 1:13

3. Psalm 101:3

4. Proverbs 23:7

5. Psalm 19:14

6. See Isaiah 26:3

7. See 2 Corinthians 10:5

8. Willard, *The Divine Conspiracy*, 334.

9. Psalm 16:11

10. See Psalm 36:8

11. Annie Dillard, *Pilgrim at Tinker Creek* (San Francisco: Harper Perennial Library).

12. Psalm 111:2

13. Psalm 46:10

14. Thomas Kelly, *A Testament of Devotion* (New York: Harper, 1941), 123–124.

15. Ken Gire, *The Reflective Life* (Colorado Springs, CO: Chariot Victor, 1998), 88.

16. Fredrich Buechner, as quoted in *Holy Sweat*, by Tim Hansel (Waco, TX: Word, 1987), 21.

17. Malachi 3:16-17

CHAPTER FIVE

1. John Calvin, as quoted in the *Jesus Discovery Bible* (San Francisco: Zondervan, 1998),1522.

2. Sweet, *SoulTsunami*, 410.

3. George Barna, *7 Habits of Highly Effective Churches* (Ventura, California: Regal Books, 2000).

4. Kathleen Norris, *Amazing Grace: A Vocaulary of Faith* (New York: Riverhead Books, 1996), 347.

5. Joseph C. Aldrich, *Gentle Persuasion*, (Portland: Multomah Press, 1988), 130.

6. Willard, *The Divine Conspiracy*, 43.

7. Matthew 16:24

8. Luke 18:22

9. John 6:53b

10. Mark 5:18

11. See Matthew 8:4.

12. John 8:11

13. John 4:10

14. Hudson Taylor, as quoted in Dr. and Mrs. Howard Taylor, *Hudson Taylor's Spiritual Secret* (Chicago: Moody Press, 1981), 172, 173.

15. P. T. Forsythe, *The Church and the Sacraments* (London: Independent Press LTD., Memorial Hall, 1917).

16. Hudson Taylor, as quoted in *Hudson Taylor's Spiritual Secret*, 156.

17. John 14:6

18. Sweet, *SoulTsunami*, 385.

19. Hudson Taylor, as quoted in *Hudson Taylor's Spiritual Secret*, 161.

20. John 15:5

21. As quoted in Eugene Peterson, *The Message*.

22. Eugene Peterson, *The Message*.

23. Paris Reidhead, *Ten Shekels and A Shirt*, a message given at Bethany Fellowship in Minneapolis, Minnesota, many years ago. This message has been called the sermon of the century. A transcribed booklet of it is available from Paris Reidhead's widow, Mrs. Marjorie Reidhead, at Bible Teaching Ministries, P.O. Box 556, Denton, Maryland, 21629. They are a faith ministry and do not attach prices to their catalog items. If ordering from them, I trust you'll be gracious to them as God directs.

24. Taken from the article by Chip Brogden, "Bring Them to Christ," posted at www.watchman.net Used by permission.

25. P. T. Forsythe, *The Person and Place of Jesus Christ* (London: Independent Press, 1930).

CHAPTER SIX

1. Dietrich Bonhoeffer, *Life Together* (San Francisco: Harper, 1978), 30, 31.

2. Ecclesiastes 4:9, 10

3. Genesis 1:26

4. See Revelation 4:11

5. See Colossians 1:16

6. C. S. Lewis, *George MacDonald Anthology* (London: Geoffrey Bles, 1945), 176, 77.

7. See 2 Samuel 15:2–6.

8. John 17:1

9. Genesis 1:26

10. E. Stanley Jones, *Christ of the Indian Road* (New York: Abingdon Press, 1925), 49.

11. Ibid.

12. See John 15:15.

CHAPTER SEVEN

1. Jean Paul Richter, as quoted in the *Jesus Discovery Bible* (San Francisco: Zondervan, 1999), 1490.

2. Calvin Miller, gen. ed., *The Book of Jesus, A Treasury of the Greatest Stories and Writing About Christ* (Touchstone Books, 1998)

3. Quote attributed to the late Richard Halverson, Chaplain of the Senate.

4. For the full text of this speech go to http://members.aol.com/circofine/red.html recorded by William L. Stone, *The Life and Times of Sa-Go-Ye-Wat-Ha, or Red Jacket* (Scholarly Press, 1970) .

5. E. Stanley Jones, *The Christ of the Indian Road.*

6. 1 Corinthians 1:23

7. E. Stanley Jones, *The Christ of the Indian Road.*

8. Ibid.

9. Ibid.

10. John 12:32

11. E. Stanley Jones, *Christ of the Indian Road*, 210.

12. Genesis 49:10

13. For the full story read Bruce Olsen's page-turner, *Bruchko* (Lake Mary, FL: Creation House, 1989), 152, 153.

CHAPTER EIGHT

1. *George MacDonald—Unspoken Sermons,* as quoted in Brent Curtis & John Eldredge, *The Sacred Romance* (Nashville: Thomas Nelson, 1997), 189.

2. Eugene H. Peterson, *The Gift—Reflections on Christian Ministry* (London: Marshall, Pickering, 1995).

3. www.24-7prayer.com. Pete Greig, used by permission.

4. Matthew 17:8

5. Francis Frangipane, *The Power of One Christlike Life,* (New Kensington, PA:, Whitaker House, 1999), 131, used by permission.

6. Statement taken from OneDay's website www.one day2000.com, about their gathering at Shelby Farms, Tennessee in the summer of 2000.

7. Eugene Peterson, *The Gift—Reflections on Christian Ministry.*

8. For a reproducible copy of this Statement of Repentance, by the author, see Appendix.

CHAPTER NINE

1. Dallas Willard, *The Divine Conspiracy*, 316.

2. 1 John 1:1-2

3. 1 Corinthians 2:4, 5

4. Luke 6:13

5. Acts 4:13

6. Karl Barth, as quoted in Tim Hansel, *Holy Sweat* (Waco, TX: Word, 1987), 26.

7. H. Wheeler Robinson, *The Christian Experience of the Holy Spirit* (London: James Nabet & Co. Ltd.,

no date), 27. As quoted in E. Stanley Jones, *The Christ of Every Road* (New York: Abingdon Press, 1930), 108.

8. Dallas Willlard, *The Divine Conspiracy*, 334.

9. Judges 5:7

10. 2 Samuel 20: 18–19

11. 1 Corinthians 4:15

12. 1 Corinthians 2:1–2.

CHAPTER TEN

1. Annie Dillard

2. Abraham Joshua Heschel, *Sabbath* (New York: Farrar, Straus and Giroux, 1951), 79.

3. Abraham Joshua Heschel, *Sabbath,* prologue.

4. Ibid.

5. 2 Thessalonians 3:10

6. Dr. Tony Campolo, Commencement address at the 108th Commencement exercise at Gordon College, Wenham, Massachusetts.

7. Matthew 11:29

8. John 5:19

9. Thomas Howard, *The Splendor of the Ordinary* (San Francisco: Ignatius Press, 2000), 13.

10. Matthew 25:37–40.

11. Abraham Joshua Heschel, *Sabbath*.

12. Brother Lawrence, *The Practice of the Presence of God (Hood and Stroughton)*.

13. Hannah Whitall Smith, *The Christian's Secret To A Happy Life* (Old Tappan, NJ: Flemming Revell 1970), 38.

14. "Moment By Moment," words by D.W. Whittle, music by May Whittle Moody, copyright 1920. Public Domain.

CHAPTER ELEVEN

1. P. T. Forsythe, *The Person and Place of Christ*, 248.

2. Revelation 22:5

3. 2 Timothy 2:12a

4. Revelation 5:9–10

5. Romans 5:17

6. Elie Wiesel, as quoted in Ken Gire, *The Reflective Life* (Colorado Springs, CO: Chariot/Victor Books, 1998).

7. Ecclesiastes 9:11

8. C. S. Lewis, *The Last Battle* (New York: Macmillan, 1956), 184.

9. Isaiah 53:3–5

10. Jean Paul Richter, as quoted in the *Jesus Discovery Bible*, 1490.

11. 2 Timothy 4:8

12. Psalm 46:1

13. John 16:33

14. 1 John 3:2

15. See Revelation 19:6, 9 and 21:7, 9, 10

16. Revelation 3:21

17. 1 Corinthians 6:2, 3

18. Paul E. Billheimer, *Destined for the Throne* (Minneapolis, Minnesota: Bethany House Publishers, 1975), 27.

19. Donald G. Mostrom, *Christians Facing the Future* (New York: Diadem Communications, 1993), 86, 87.

20. David Bryant, *The Hope At Hand* (Grand Rapids, MI: Baker, 1996), 53.

Afterword

1. Adrian Rogers, the *Jesus Discovery Bible* (Grand Rapids, MI: Zondervan, 1999).

Acknowledgements

A. W. Tozer loved to tell the story about the donkey that carried Jesus into Jerusalem. Tozer mused about what might have gone through the donkey's mind as he saw jackets cast before him, palm branches waving warm welcomes as he approached. "Ah, at last, I am getting the recognition I deserve. Finally, I am being given my rightful place of honor." We smile at the poor donkey's cluelessness, but we are like him whenever we think "it is all about us." At our best, we are merely carriers of Jesus.

Yet in the holy reciprocity of God, *we* too end up being carried by the love of others. I have been buoyed through life by rich, sure-footed love. My dear husband Joey has for twenty-five years poured nothing but strong and constant encouragement into me. My son Joel warms my heart and gives me hope by his sheer existence. Virginia Smith and Virginia Otis faithfully have carried me in prayer.

There is a long line of men and women who wrote their passion for Jesus in deafening words that have thundered through my days: E. Stanley Jones, Hudson Taylor, Hannah Whitall Smith, Roy and Revell Hession, Brother

Lawrence, and many others. I have been nourished at deep wells by forward-thinking friends who never tire of talking about Jesus—Lynn McMahan, Celia and Stuart McAlpine, Lynn Heatley, and Hilary Young. Through them, God has loved me wonderfully.

This little book found its way into your hands because Beth Clark of Thomas Nelson Publishers introduced me to Victor Oliver, a Jesus man who just happens to be an editor as well. Thank you, Beth and Victor, for opening a door for this book. May a wide door to God's heart be opened for you.

And thank you, dear reader. May these words ravish your heart with the all-encompassing passion God has for His Son. My prayer is that this will be simply one more match that ignites that sacred flame.

About the Author

Fawn Parish serves on the executive board of the Internat'l Reconciliation Coalition comprised of ministries that promote reconciliation among gender, race, sectarian divisions, and societies. She serves as the national worship leader for Lydia Prayer Fellowship Internat'l, a group of praying women from 80 countries. Fawn co-leads Pray Ventura, and she is the founder and director of Concerts of Prayer in Ventura County. As a speaker at conferences, retreats, and churches, Fawn desires to instill in audiences a greater thirst for Jesus. She is the author of *Honor* and a contributing writer to the *Women of Destiny Bible*. Fawn has produced and written a series of mission videos, including The *40/40 Window for Adults*, The *10/40 Window for Kids* and *Prayerwalking for Kids*. She has also produced several music resources that include *No Boundaries* and *It's All About You*. Fawn is a wife, mother, and a passionate lover of Jesus.

Read these other inspiring books written by women with a heart for Christ:

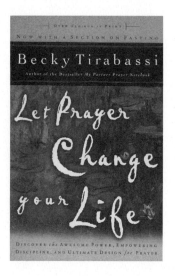

Let Prayer Change Your Life: Discover the Awesome Power, Empowering Discipline, and Ultimate Design for Prayer, by Becky Tirabassi. This book has already been read by over 250,000 people, and the consensus is that reading and applying its instruction will change your life. Practical, applicable, and encouraging, this book helps you discover what prayer really is—a conversation between two people who love each other. ISBN: 0-7852-6885-5

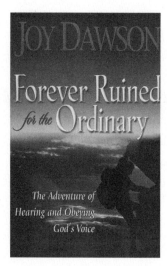

Forever Ruined for the Ordinary: The Adventure of Hearing and Obeying God's Voice, by Joy Dawson. Joy Dawson describes what happened when she decided to follow God with an obedient heart: "I was tuned in and turned on to God, the Creator and Sustainer of the universe. I took off on an adventure of a lifetime… hearing and obeying God's voice. I was forever ruined for the ordinary." Emphasizing God's commitment to be personally involved in our lives, Joy shares the lessons of a lifetime of faithful obedience to God. Through stories and biblical teaching, she helps readers discover the excitement of learning how to listen to God, joyfully obey Him, and see the wonder of the results that follow. ISBN: 0-7852-6608-9